Dos and Don'ts in Human Resources Management

D0325442

Matthias Zeuch

Editor

Dos and Don'ts in Human Resources Management

A Practical Guide

 Springer Gabler

Editor
Matthias Zeuch
Beijing
China

ISBN 978-3-662-43552-6   ISBN 978-3-662-43553-3 (eBook)
DOI 10.1007/978-3-662-43553-3
Springer Heidelberg New York Dordrecht London

Library of Congress Control Number: 2014950911

Printed on acid-free paper

Springer is part of Springer Science + Business Media (www.springer.com)

Initial Remarks

"Keeping IT Short and Simple"—this principle is not easy to follow when it comes to Human Resources Management. But, this group of experienced HR leaders and experts gave it a try—and it worked excellent!

All authors focus on clear advice from practice to practice, providing the reader with immediate value-added for his or her work in HR management.

Can such advice be debated? Yes, and all authors look forward to your comments in the LinkedIn Forum "KISS HRM—Keep IT Short and Simple in HR Management"!

As an experienced HR leader, the reader may use this book as reference when designing new programs or reviewing existing HR practices.

As HR employee, the reader will get a comprehensive overview of all areas of HR management from the operational side.

As a person interested in working for HR, the book serves as career orientation, informing the reader which topics HR deals with in real-life.

For all those who want to reflect the subjects in a more detailed way and those who want to learn from practice examples, this team of authors currently also produces the "Handbook of Human Resources Management", which will be published by Springer Science+Business Media in 2015.

My thanks go to all authors of this book and their families—the authors for spending their anyway scarce recreational time to write the articles and their families for tolerating and supporting it.

Beijing   Matthias Zeuch.
June 2014

Contents

Part V   Compensation and Benefits

Part VI   Administration and Payroll

Contributors

Rainer Allinger Berlin, Germany
Laurence Baltzer Berlin, Germany
Bernhard Balz Nuertingen, Germany
Kerstin Beckers Berlin, Germany
Nora Binder Vienna, Austria
Julia Borggraefe Berlin, Germany
Sandy Chen Shenzhen, China
Soo May Cheng Sydney, Australia
Jürgen Czajor Beijing, China
Nicole Dessain Evanston, IL, USA
John Dijk Mandaluyong City, Philippines
William Eggers Frankfurt am Main, Germany
Lisa Emerson Glen Ellyn, IL, USA
Eric Engesaeth Amsterdam, Netherlands
Pirkko Erichsen Stuttgart, Germany
Ute Gallmeister Berlin, Germany
Michael Griffitts San Francisco, CA, USA
Oliver Grohmann Singapore, Singapore
Thomas Gruhle Frankfurt am Main, Germany
Heike Hartrath Berlin, Germany
Thomas Haussmann Frankfurt am Main, Germany
Ulrike Hildebrand Chicago, IL, USA
Andreas Hofmann Frankfurt am Main, Germany
Karen Hughey Overland Park, KS, USA
Maureen Hunter Armonk, NY, USA
Lorenz Illing Berlin, Germany
Eckart Jensen Singapore, Singapore

Nicola Mackin Stuttgart, Germany
Karen Minor West Bloomfield, MI, USA
Brian Moll Brooklyn, NY, USA
Jens Peisert Berlin, Germany
Sylke Piéch Berlin, Germany
Yvonne Prang Munich, Germany
James Purvis Genève, Switzerland
Konrad Reiher Bad Camberg, Germany
Rainer Schaetzle Wilen, Switzerland
Janina Schönebeck Berlin, Germany
Manfred Schönebeck Berlin, Germany
Lynn Schuster Wilton, CT, USA
Carla K. Shull Denver, CO, USA
Olaf B. Tietz Berlin, Germany
Agnes Tse Shanghai, China
Christian Weiss Lampertheim, Germany
Rainer Wieland Gaggenau, Germany
Josef Wieland Friedrichshafen, Germany
Matthias Zeuch Central, Hong Kong

Authors' Profiles

Dr. Rainer Allinger has 28 years of work experience in the services industry, mainly financial services and sales within globally acting DAX 30 group. Studies and doctorate in jurisprudence. Professional experience in HR as labor law consultant, head of centers of competence for HR policies, HR development and Executive Management, covering business units in Europe, Africa and Asia. Currently HR-Business Partner and Executive Committee member for HR.

Laurence Baltzer, Consulting and Coaching, Berlin/Germany, has 22 years of HR experience in large international companies. She grew up in France, has been living in Germany for 27 years, studied Business Administration and has been working in an international context since then. Before setting up her own company, she was in charge of the Europe Team of the Daimler Corporate Academy (Qualification, Training, Coaching). She has additional education in Training, Coaching and Mediation.

Bernhard Balz heads the department "Audit Human Resources" at a major company in automotive industry. After his 18-year career in various capacities in the automotive industry, especially in Information Technology, Sales & Marketing, Controlling and Human Resources, he moved to the audit function as a supervisor (senior manager) starting auditing Sales & Marketing and now auditing Human Resources Departments and Human Resources Functions worldwide.

Kerstin Beckers is Manager Executive HRD at Daimler Financial Services AG, Germany. As Manager Executive HRD, Kerstin Beckers is responsible for HR development and succession planning for the Daimler Financial Services top management worldwide. After finishing her master's degree in business administration, Kerstin Beckers started her professional career with Daimler Financial Services AG. She has been working in different areas of HR Management with focus on global people development, leadership performance, potential management, compliance and expatriate management.

Nora Binder is an experienced international human resources professional, with a passion for working in multicultural environments and exploring different approaches to human capital management. In Vienna she has recently contributed with her expertise to the UN Organisation CTBTO as HR Training Consultant. During her 10 years in China, she was assigned Head of Human Resources, Training and Recruiting at the German Industry and Commerce Greater China in Beijing. Prior to this appointment, Ms. Binder was People Development Manager at the Industrial Solutions Division (IS) of Siemens Ltd. China.

Dr. Julia Borggraefe is Head of HR at Messe Berlin and partner at Autenticon—Consulting In Context. Dr. Borggraefe has 14 years of experience in HR Management, and within those 14 years, 9 were also in HR compliance. On the one hand, she is a lawyer and has a strong legal background; at the same time she is experienced HR manager (e.g. senior manager for the Western European HR department of Daimler; senior vice president HR & corporate governance Messe Berlin) and educated as mediator, systemic consultant and change manager and built up HR compliance for the European HR department at Daimler.

Sandy Chen is the HR Director of Great China from Orbotech Limited. Sandy holds an MBA degree from Shanghai University of Finance and Economics; she has engaged in HR management for more than 16 years and has solid experience in each HR function. With her strong leadership and professional HR background, she has achieved great impacts on both business and organization. Sandy has introduced the skill inventory concept to the organization and adopted to the engineers professionalism certification program in whole pacific.

Dr. Soo-May Cheng is Associate Professor and Deputy Dean, Sydney Campus of the Asia Pacific International College in Australia. She teaches and supervises graduate students in human resource management, international business, cross-cultural management, research methodology and other areas. She is responsible for the curricular development, delivery and quality assurance of business management courses in the Master of Business Management programs. She also oversees the human resource affairs and the academic research agenda of the College, as well as assist with regulatory compliance in all academic matters.

Jürgen Czajor After graduating from the University of Konstanz, Jürgen has been working for Daimler more than 30 years in various Human Resources functions. He started as a Human Resources Consultant in the truck plants in Kassel and Gaggenau, before he was promoted to management in the Headquarters in Stuttgart where he worked on Human Resources Policy, Corporate Organization and for Daimler Corporate University. In 2003 he was seconded to Tokyo on an international assignment to support the Joint Venture with Mitsubishi-Fuso in all Human Resources related items. In 2008 he moved to Beijing where he took over leading positions in the field of operational Human Resources and International Assignment Management.

Nicole Dessain is the Founder of talent.imperative, a next generation talent management consultancy that supports clients' ability to execute their strategic plan through sustainable talent management by providing HR and operational leaders with actionable consulting, insightful research, and execution-oriented coaching around their most pressing talent challenges. Nicole is an Accenture-trained consultant and talent management thought leader with over a decade of global experience advising HR and business leaders on their talent strategy and people programs.

John van Dijk is a Dutch national and a world citizen. After working as a teacher for 5 years, since 1980 he has been leading organizations and people. At first mainly in sports governing bodies and governmental surroundings and later in professional sport, hospitality, consulting and training and manufacturing industry. He is founder and owner of Macom Consultancy BV and Pacific Leader Development Ltd. John has worked in The Netherlands, Belgium, France, Germany, China and The Philippines.

William Eggers leads Hay Group's Executive Rewards Practice in Germany. He works with top executives and supervisory board members on executive reward solutions. Prior to joining Hay Group, William has been the global head for compensation at Linde and worked for Daimler Financial Services in different roles in Germany and the USA. He started his career as a consultant for executive pay and worked in this role for many major global organizations. William holds a degree in business administration.

Lisa Emerson is Vice President—Global Total Compensation for McDonald's Corporation. Lisa has responsibility for all aspects of McDonald's compensation and benefits strategy and execution globally. This includes executive and broad based compensation, expatriate and stock plan policy, health and welfare, and retirement benefits. In addition, she executes fiduciary responsibilities and interacts regularly with the McDonald's Compensation Committee of the Board of Directors.

Assoc. Prof. Dr. Eric Engesaeth is Director & NL Head of Executive Reward with Hay Group, the Netherlands and member of the global Executive Reward Leadership of Hay Group. He consults with international companies on executive board, supervisory board, and senior management remuneration. Clients include all industry sectors. Eric Engesaeth is currently Associate Professor Managerial Compensation at TIAS School for Business and Society. He is, among others, author of the books "Fundamenten van bestuurdersbeloning" (2008) and "Managerial Compensation Contracting" (2011).

Pirkko Erichsen is Senior Manager HR Development and Business Procedures at Daimler Financial Services AG, Germany. Main professional experience: Performance and Potential Management, Talent Management, Executive Development, HR Management, Diversity and Culture, HR Reporting and Controlling. Studies: Education, Major Organizational Development and Media Education. International Experience: 5 years HR Key Account Management Singapore, Region Africa and Asia Pacific.

Ute Gallmeister is Vice Director at Institute for Transfer of Innovations and Project Management of International Academy gGmbH at Free University Berlin, Member of Managing Board E.R.P. GmbH. Core competencies: transfer of innovation from idea generation to implementation • method development and application • CRM • brand development and positioning • communication design and product communication. Education: Dipl.-Betriebswirt B.A.

Michael Griffitts is currently a Senior Manager, Global Leadership and Employee Development for the Roche Group where he supports global talent management and leadership development. Originally from California, Michael completed graduate work in Social Psychology at Columbia University, and has worked for Roche in New Jersey, Switzerland, and currently lives in the San Francisco Bay Area with his wife and three children.

Oliver Grohmann currently is the HR Senior VP for the Mercedes-Benz Car Group Overseas region. Managing the HR activities in 22 countries, he has over 16 years of expertise as a HR practitioner. After starting his career as a lawyer, he moved on to the HR profession in Lufthansa before joining Daimler in 1999. He took on various responsibilities including Expat Management, C&B, HR Controlling, Talent Management, Head of HR and also has extensive experience in the area of Change Management.

Thomas Gruhle is a member of the Hay Group DACH Management Team. In this role Thomas is responsible for the standardized product & services business in the areas of compensation & benefits, talent management/diagnostics and employee surveys. Thomas is advising global and national organizations from various industries to make informed decisions about their reward strategies by providing insightful compensation & benefits information. Thomas is also responsible for data collection process and quality assurance of the total remuneration database of Hay Group in Germany and Austria.

Dr. Heike Hartrath has 16 years of professional experience and is currently head of a cross-regional Payroll Outsourcing Project covering a total of 30 countries and almost 100 legal entities in Europe and Asia. Heike holds a Ph.D. in American, British and German Studies. As a former Ghostwriter she has a background in Communications and looks back at 12 years of different management roles in HR, covering areas from Marketing and Recruiting to HR Development and Payroll. She has worked both in global headquarters as well as in Europe and Asia.

Dr. Thomas Haussmann is Senior Vice President and Practice Leader Reward at Hay Group Germany/Austria/Switzerland, Frankfurt. Thomas has been a consultant for more than 20 years and is the author of two books and various articles on reward-related issues.

Ulrike Hildebrand is an internationally experienced Human Resources Executive with dual citizenship in the USA and Germany. She has a degree in economics from Carl-von-Ossietzky Universitaet in Oldenburg, Germany with majors in Strategic Business Management, Human Resources Management and Industrial/ Organizational Psychology and spent 10+years successfully leading HR teams in the automotive industry.

Andreas Hofmann is Managing Partner at Hoyck Management Consultants since 2011. He has over 16 years of experience in international HR functions, amongst others as Head of Compensation & Mobility and Head of HR for the corporate Headquarter at Bilfinger SE and Head of Executive & Equity Compensation at SAP AG.

Karen Hughey's career spans more than 20 years. Karen has experience in all aspects of Human Resources primarily with Fortune 500 companies. She recently established an HR Department from the ground up when a small company acquired a larger one necessitating a formal HR Department. There she successfully launched organizational development and change management programs resulting in increased leadership effectiveness. She has worked as a training and HR consultant for companies in the USA and Canada. She is also a college adjunct instructor.

Dr. Maureen Hunter's expertise is in organizational change and leadership development. She currently works for IBM identifying and developing business and technical leaders. Prior to IBM Maureen's consulting work encompassed strategic approaches to diversity, change readiness, organizational culture, and transformation. Maureen earned a B.S. in Organizational Behavior from Yale, an M.A. in Organizational Psych from Columbia, and an M.A. in Clinical Psych and a Ph.D. in Social Psych from Georgia State University.

Lorenz Illing is Partner at i-potentials, the HR Consultancy for the European digital world. As Director of the direct search division Digital Executives in Berlin, Lorenz and his team of highly specialized Consultants deliver what every scaling start-up, every established Internet company, VC or seasoned corporation needs for long-term market growth and success: Entrepreneurial leaders and digital experts who are able to shape the future.

Eckart Jensen studied Public Administration, Economics and Business Administration and has 30 years of international experience in Audit, Business Consulting, Transformation Management, Executive Development and HR Operations. He spent one-third of his professional life in Asia and settled down in Singapore in 2007. After 24 years with Daimler he decided to leave the Group and founded HR ACT Pte Ltd. The company offers HR Advisory Services (HR Compliance and HR Audit) and HR Operations Support for small companies, supporting organizations to get their HR Operations 100% compliant.

Nicola Mackin is currently a Senior HR Manager Mercedes Benz Cars Overseas with 15 years of HR experience in the automotive industry and in HR consultancy firms. Nicola holds an M.A. in Anthropology, Psychology and Communications as well as a Diploma in Economics. During her career, she has filled various management roles in all major fields of HR—operational, strategic and at project level; both in global headquarters as well as in the field (Europe, Asia Africa Pacific).

Karen Minor is Owner and CEO of Talent Works, LLC. Her firm offers Talent Management solutions and clients include global companies in financial services and automotive, pharmaceutical and retail. Karen has led teams in the development and delivery of Performance Management, Recruiting, Coaching, and On-boarding, Mentoring, Succession Planning, Training and Leadership Development. Karen earned a MBA from National University and a Bachelor's degree in Human Development from Wayne State University.

Brian Moll is accomplished Talent Acquisition Director with a strong focus in partnering with top organizations within Marketing/Communications, Technology, Ecommerce, and Media. Highly regarded as a collaborative recruiting enthusiast that brings a track record of building and leading progressive recruiting teams. He graduated from Missouri State University as B.A. Communications/Marketing and gained experience as recruiter e.g. at Universal McCann.

Jens Peisert is Partner and Managing Director of E.R.P. GmbH • Company owner of Jens Peisert Vertriebe. Ten years experience as managing director of Swiss consumer products and drugs company • 20 years experience as consultant in leading functions in international consultancies. Core competencies: goal-oriented business management • diagnosis and creative therapy of existential risks for business development • use of the high developed common sense for solving all ranges of problems.

Dr. Sylke Piéch is director of Institute for International Human Resource Management at the International Academy for Innovative Pedagogy, Psychology and Economics at the Free University of Berlin. Her areas of expertise are: personnel & leadership development, international talent development, coaching & team management, optimization of foreign deployment processes and facilitating effective corporate communications structures.

Yvonne Prang is a Senior Department Head at McDonald's and leads the Compensation & Benefits and People Systems teams of one of the largest global brands in Germany. With her team, she provides ideas, frameworks and processes as well as the IT-solutions to recruit, to motivate, and to retain the company's key asset, its employees. Her prior work experience includes various roles at Infineon Technologies, Kienbaum Management Consultants, PriceWaterhouseCoopers and Siemens. Yvonne holds an MBA from the USA and postgraduate degrees from France and Germany.

James Purvis is head of Talent Acquisition at CERN. He has over 20 years' experience in modernization and process improvement, working with web technologies from their inception. In 2007 James joined the HR management team in implementing CERN's modern HR strategy. Passionate about recruitment, he strives to modernize, innovate and make a difference. Achieving great science requires great skills, and James team's challenge is to find, attract & select the skills CERN requires for today and tomorrow.

Dr. Konrad Reiher As one of Hay Group's leading global experts in Job Evaluation and the different applications like organizational clarity and effectiveness, pay and value alignment, etc. Konrad works with a number of international and national clients since more than 20 years. He has supported clients and colleagues on organizational effectiveness and on translating organizational models into needed roles, pay levels and reward systems. Konrad has a diploma in Mathematics & Physics and a Ph.D. in Mathematics from University of Paderborn, Germany.

Rainer Schaetzle Global Head Performance Management & Recognition, at F. Hoffmann-La Roche, Basel—Switzerland. Established global recognition program at Roche servicing close to 200 affiliates in 140 countries with over 80,000 employees participating on one common platform. Management experience: Global Rewards and Performance Management at Zurich Financial Services and Allianz Group • Human Capital Practice of Arthur Andersen in Germany.

Janina Schönebeck is a Senior Consultant and Project Leader E.R.P. GmbH. Core competencies: international and intercultural management • communication design • international marketing • market research • consumer behavior • satisfaction research • industrial and organizational psychology. Education: Dipl. Kauffrau.

Manfred Schönebeck is a Partner of E. R. P. GmbH • Chancellor of Carl Benz Academy • psychotherapist with own praxis • managing partner and director of Institute for Transfer of Innovations and Project Management of International Academy gGmbH at Free University Berlin. Core competencies: communication research • creative and perceptive processes • behavioral, medial and organizational psychology • experimental research, cognition, emotions and motivation. Education: Dipl. Psychologe.

Lynn Schuster is an Executive Coach/Trusted Advisor/Organization Consultant. Lynn is an Executive Leadership and Organizational Coach/Consultant who works with top of the house C-suite executives. Lynn spent 11 years with IBM subsequent to her time as Managing Director of a boutique consulting firm focused on Executive Coaching, Assessment, Acquisition Integration, Leadership, Strategy Alignment and Executive Leadership Development. Major clients were included in the Fortune 100 companies.

Dr. Carla K. Shull leads Global HR Effectiveness at Arrow Electronics managing improvement of human resources processes and tools to increase the efficiency and effectiveness of delivering solutions to the business. Carla's M.S. and Ph.D. in Industrial/Organizational Psychology launched her career as an internal and external consultant working with Fortune 500 companies in all facets of HR specializing in determining effective selection methods and showing business impact of those methods.

Olaf B. Tietz is Managing Director at Carl Benz Academy—First Global Cloud Academy GmbH and Director of Institute for Innovation Transfer and Project Management of the International Academy at the Free University Berlin. Core competencies: innovative project design, segmentation in luxury customer segments, emotional-feedback-interviews, development of innovative products, internet, TV and radio advertisements and photography, research of emotions.

Agnes Tse is currently the Vice President, Human Resources, Asia Pacific of a US industrial company which has US\$ 23 billion revenue. She is now based at Shanghai. She is providing strategic HR functional leadership across the Asia Pacific region at this company. Agnes is originally from Hong Kong. She has lived and worked in Shanghai for more than 10 years. She has held senior HR positions in companies like WR Grace and Philips at China. She has indepth knowledge of HR practices in China as well as the Asia Pacific region. Agnes is also a certified executive coach.

Christian Weiss is an experienced project manager and expert in organizational transformation and workforce planning and optimization. He consults global corporations and midsize organization. Christian is leading Hay Group's "Building Effective Organizations" Practice in Germany. He started his career at Unisys Corporation, later working as a partner in a boutique consulting group in Germany. Christian holds a Master degree in Business Administration from the University of Regensburg.

Rainer Wieland started his career with a 3 years apprenticeship as toolmaker. After that, worked in the die maker maintenance in an automotive manufacturing plant in South-West Germany for 12 years. He became responsible for process planning in the machinery section. Two years later he joined the vocational education center of the plant as Master Trainer. Eight years ago Rainer took an international assignment in China. First, he established a vocational training system and is now responsible for Blue Collar training in a large automotive manufacturing plant in Beijing.

Prof. Dr. Josef Wieland is the Director of the Leadership Excellence Institute at the Zeppelin University, Friedrichshafen. Prior to this, he was the Professor of Business Administration at the University of Applied Sciences Konstanz, and continues to be the Director of its Doctoral program. His expertise in the field of Compliance and Business Ethics for decades has been honored with several awards. He is an adviser and compliance monitor for the World Bank. In 2014 his latest book "Governance Ethics: Global Value Creation, Economic Organization and Normativity" will be published.

Matthias Zeuch is Founder and CEO of HRMnext, an international academy and consulting company, driving excellence in HR management. Matthias has more than 25 years of experience in HR, thereof 15 years in upper management positions in North America, Europe and Asia/Pacific for Daimler/Mercedes-Benz including membership in regional management boards.

Part I
HR Marketing and Recruiting

Introduction

Nicole Dessain

HR Marketing

HR Marketing includes activities that attract active and passive candidates who exhibit the company's desired skills and behaviors.

HR Marketing should be based on a clearly defined and well communicated Employer Value Proposition (EVP) which is a set of positioning statements outlining why the company is an attractive employer.

Recruiting

Recruiting activities are geared towards hiring people who are interested in the company and who have the skills and behaviors needed to successfully perform their role.

The recruiting process is comprised of sourcing the candidate, pre-assessment, final selection, job offer and contracting.

While HR activities are usually internally focused, "HR Marketing and Recruiting" clearly has an external focus. The way the company presents itself as an

N. Dessain (✉)
Evanston, IL, USA
e-mail: DosDontsHR@yahoo.com

© Springer-Verlag Berlin Heidelberg 2015
M. Zeuch (ed.), *Dos and Don'ts in Human Resources Management*,
DOI 10.1007/978-3-662-43553-3_1

employer through its HR Marketing has a major impact on the overall company image.

Recruiting has an impact on the company's reputation:

- Job postings indicate growth and optimism regarding the future.
- The level of respect and courtesy the company expresses to people who applied but were not selected reveals the real values of the company and its culture.
- Job applicants share their experiences of the selection process via social media—the good and the bad.
- Candidates may be company's current or future customers.

Employer Branding

Matthias Zeuch

First: Analyze Competition

Analyze how your major competitors have positioned their employer brands.

Customize Messages

Customize your HR marketing messages to your target groups and align creative artwork with those messages.

Address Directly

Address people directly in HR marketing messages (for example, not "It is great to work at ABC," but "Come to ABC because we have great jobs for you").

M. Zeuch (✉)
Beijing, China
e-mail: DosDontsHR@yahoo.com

© Springer-Verlag Berlin Heidelberg 2015
M. Zeuch (ed.), *Dos and Don'ts in Human Resources Management,*
DOI 10.1007/978-3-662-43553-3_2

Allow Local Differences

(For multi-national companies) Allow country-specific differences to employer brands—unless you have a highly internationalized team of people who frequently rotate among countries, in this case, having only one global employer brand makes sense.

Make a Project Plan

Developing an employer brand—if done right—is a major effort. It demands a large time commitment from HR and also from interviewees, participants in focus groups. Resources must be planned and committed in advance.

Don't Make it an "HR Thing"

Do not start on an employer branding project if you feel that management is not committed to the employer branding effort. If the employer brand is seen by management as "just an HR thing" or a "hobby of the HR leader", it will not have any real-life effects. An honest commitment by management is the prerequisite for any successful employer branding.

Digital Recruiting

James Purvis

Don't Simply Map Existing Processes to a New Technology

Technology is an enabler. To get the most out of new technologies, rethink your HR/recruiting process. Don't simply take your existing ways of recruiting and map them onto the new technology. New technology allows for new approaches to your recruitment process to increase quality, reduce costs or become more competitive. Implementing technology successfully will, however, require a change in mind-set and a rethink of your existing recruiting processes.

Treat the Candidate as Your Customer/Understand Your Target Audience

See your process from your target audience's point of view. Treat each potential candidate as a customer. Understand their behavior. Profile them. Then prioritize your implementation of technology around what adds the most value first.

J. Purvis (✉)
Genève, Switzerland
e-mail: DosDontsHR@yahoo.com

© Springer-Verlag Berlin Heidelberg 2015
M. Zeuch (ed.), *Dos and Don'ts in Human Resources Management*,
DOI 10.1007/978-3-662-43553-3_3

Define Metrics

The old adage says you can not manage what you don't measure and this is equally true for digital recruiting. Measure your impact and your engagement of social media and use of technology. Invest in those giving highest returns and consider dropping those not making results. Make your decisions based on metrics instead of fashions.

Take Decisions Based on Data, Not on Opinions

Don't fall into the trap of designing a new career website based on battle of 'Hippos' (Highest-Important-Paid-Person's Opinions). Use data to make decisions. Implement the features that are the most sought-after by your target population.

Design a Strategy

Digital recruiting offers an overwhelming choice in opportunities. Which social media channel? What applicant tracking system (ATS)? Before embarking on any implementation of any component, paint the big picture and agree on an overall strategy.

Identify and Implement Some Quick Wins with Technology

Some technology projects can have long timescales and require big budgets; others can be implemented in less than a day. Before embarking on the former, build confidence by identifying some quick wins with the technology in order to create confidence and trust in your strategy.

Understand When You Do and Don't Need In-house IT

With the ubiquity of Saas (Software as a Service) solutions available in HR you may have more autonomy than you realise for implementing technology. You may, however, have existing corporate systems or processes which require interfaces. Understand the role of our in-house IT team but also the opportunity of off-the-shelf Saas services in recruitment.

Be Aware of Technology Paradigm Shifts and the Hype Cycle

Don't assume that the technology you have just implemented today will be valid in 5 years' time. Within 10 years it may certainly be obsolete. The exponential growth in mobile means your current way of applying may have to be entirely rethought to leverage mobile opportunities. Your existing traditional career website may be gone in a few years.

Monitor the Trends and Stay Up to Date

Technology is changing tremendously, providing regularly new opportunities. Keep up to date with news-feeds on what is hot and what is not and question what potential role these new technologies could play in a recruitment or sourcing process.

Recruiting Events

Nicole Dessain

Seize Marketing Opportunity

Use recruiting events both for HR marketing and for recruiting. Invest in a professional look and feel for the exhibition stands, print material and possibly video equipment to show company movie/company presentation, etc.

Treat all Applicants with Equal Respect

Create a positive experience for those visiting your event or your booth at a larger event for ALL, not only for those whom you want to hire. Remember: they all are ambassadors of your company's employer image.

Keep Conversations Short

Try to limit conversations with interested visitors to 5 min maximum. Schedule more in-depth interviews for after the event.

N. Dessain (✉)
Evanston, IL, USA
e-mail: DosDontsHR@yahoo.com

© Springer-Verlag Berlin Heidelberg 2015
M. Zeuch (ed.), *Dos and Don'ts in Human Resources Management,*
DOI 10.1007/978-3-662-43553-3_4

Involve Hiring Managers

Involve managers from the hiring departments during the event. Make sure you have enough administrative support during the event.

Don't Assume all Audiences are Alike

Think through which type of events and collaborations are most effective for various functions and geographies.

Don't Underestimate Organizational Effort

All types of recruiting events require pre-planning and post-event follow-up in addition to managing the actual event day.

Don't Underestimate Information Capturing

Don't underestimate the challenge and importance of capturing information about candidates during the event for an effective follow up.

Don't Forget to Include Technology in the Event

For Recruiting Events to be successful in the age of social media, ensure you include tablets, apps, and other technology as part of the event.

University Relationships

Soo May Cheng

Invest in Relationships

A total commitment to bilateral partnership would mean that engagement should occur at all levels of both organizations, from CEO down through to lower ranks. Endorsement by top executives should signal a willingness to establish links at departmental levels, including student and alumni groups. Consortiums and networks of partners are also popular collaborative structures. The test of commitment is the investment of time, liaison personnel and funds to cultivate these relationships.

Be Mindful of Compliance Aspects

Where universities or their partners are public entities, there are possibly stricter compliance rules that must be observed. With the cost of doing business and the risks of partnership escalating, private organizations must also be prudent with their investments in collaborative ventures. Hence it is good practice to observe accountability, transparency and due process in all transactions.

S. M. Cheng (✉)
Sydney, Australia
e-mail: DosDontsHR@yahoo.com

© Springer-Verlag Berlin Heidelberg 2015
M. Zeuch (ed.), *Dos and Don'ts in Human Resources Management,*
DOI 10.1007/978-3-662-43553-3_5

Cultivate Win–Win Attitudes and Behavior

When partners approach any joint project unselfishly, taking into consideration the others' interests as well as their own, there is a much better chance of success and achievement of all parties' objectives. Tangibly, this translates into sharing of information, facilities, personnel, expertise and other organizational assets.

Appoint a Liaison Officer

Appoint a liaison officer on each side to manage the communication that flows between the partners. The role of coordinator is critical in ensuring that information is channeled to appropriate persons, that any query and request is followed through properly, and that all communication emanating from each party will be consistent. This liaison person must be fairly senior so as to command respect and to be able to access all channels within his/her own organization. He/she must have some expertise relevant to the role, and have strong interpersonal skills.

Do Not Overlook Less Well-known Universities or Companies as Partners

These organizations may not command the same star value as ivy-league universities or Fortune 500 companies, but may be able to demonstrate more flexibility and commitment to a partnership. There may also be better strategic fit between universities and businesses in correspondingly similar "tiers" in their respective sectors.

Do Not Be Limited in the Scope of Collaboration

As universities evolve to become more managerial and entrepreneurial, while business leaders acquire more scholarly perspectives through further education, the areas of common interest are bound to increase. Extending collaboration beyond one project, e.g. a company hiring graduates from its partner university, deepens a partnership and makes it more enduring.

Do Not Let a Partnership Terminate with the Departure of Individuals Who have Initially Championed It

Often, collaboration founded on the charismatic or visionary leaders' initial commitment does not outlive the leaders' departure from their organizations. With mobility of professors and business executives increasing in more turbulent socioeconomic environments, it is essential that mechanisms be set up to give the partnerships stability and continuity. Institutionalizing collaboration through formal agreements, liaison offices or joint project teams will extend the life of the partnership beyond the influence of their initiators.

Employee Referral Programs

Brian Moll

General Advice

Before implementing an employee referral program (ERP) at your company, provide HR and Finance Leadership with extensive research on best practice and prospectus on possible expense and maintenance. It is important to assess multiple ERP programs within different types of industries to gauge, which is the right approach for your organization.

Consider Non-Monetary Rewards

Not all ERP programs require monetary rewards for successful referral hires. Recognition from internal leadership, event access with thought leaders i.e. conferences/workshops, and additional time off can be used as reward for participating. This approach provides further employee betterment, networking, and learning opportunities that can produce higher quality employment experience vs. just getting money.

B. Moll (✉)
Brooklyn, NY, USA
e-mail: DosDontsHR@yahoo.com

© Springer-Verlag Berlin Heidelberg 2015
M. Zeuch (ed.), *Dos and Don'ts in Human Resources Management*,
DOI 10.1007/978-3-662-43553-3_6

Year Round ERP and Unlimited Referrals

Recruiting is a year round activity that requires employees to be incentivized to assist in the continual identification of strong passive candidates that are in the market and could be referred for current and future opportunities. ERP's should be year round and no cap put on the amount of referrals employees can submit. Each referral should be tagged and if they are successfully hired anytime in the future, a referral fee should be paid out to the successful employee who referred that candidate.

Break Payments into Installments

If possible, break ERP payments into installments to confirm referrals have successfully been employed for an acceptable period of time. This also helps retain employees who are responsible for the referral.

Continuous Management and Promotion of ERP

It is important to continually promote and highlight ERP details and advantages of participation to employees. The best times to introduce the program are: during new hire orientation, company meetings, and scheduled times during the year. Showcase how easy it is to participate and what the rewards look like on a regular basis.

Fluctuating Rewards and Schedule

In an effort to keep employee populations attention and interest in ERP, it is important to run promotional periods where successful referrals are paid a premium award vs. the normal amounts. This will help keep interest in program participation during key quarters of hiring growth.

Internship Management

Michael Griffitts

Use Internships for Long-Term Recruiting

Use internships to observe talent and motivation of the interns ("real-life assessment"). This enhances the quality of hiring decisions and lowers the risk of attrition in the first year of employment. Both the intern and the company know "what they will get."

Use Internships to Freshen Up Your Company Culture

Use the ideas and new forms of communication of interns to stay in touch with the new generation entering the labor market. Design activities that will combine business relevance and idea generation (e.g. hack-a-thons). Encourage interns to bring ideas and energy into the culture of the organization.

M. Griffitts (✉)
San Francisco, CA, USA
e-mail: DosDontsHR@yahoo.com

© Springer-Verlag Berlin Heidelberg 2015
M. Zeuch (ed.), *Dos and Don'ts in Human Resources Management,*
DOI 10.1007/978-3-662-43553-3_7

Combine with University Relationships

Use existing university relationships or build new ones to develop a sustainable pipeline for internships. Potentially, combine internships with research in the university (e.g. doctorate internships, master thesis internships) to create a win-win situation for the university and the company.

Don't Use as a Low-Cost Capacity

Although interns usually cost significantly less cost than regular employees, do not ignore the educational purpose of the internship and view them as additional operational workers. It could be a violation of labor laws, union agreements and other forms of applicable regulations. Treating interns solely as an extra pair of hands can negatively influence the company's image as an employer in relevant parts of the labor market (including interns' personal and social media communities!) and could certainly also reduce the number of future interns who view the company as attractive.

Engage Senior Leaders and High Potentials

Create opportunities for senior leaders to interact with interns as part of on-boarding activities or for lunch-and-learn sessions. Use high potentials as managers and mentors to give them additional experience in managing and developing others. This can have an energizing effect on the leaders and the high-potentials, and the interns will appreciate the exposure to leadership and the learning benefits of high-quality managers.

Trainee Programs

Soo May Cheng

Be Certain There Is Need for Trainees

Discuss intensively within the organization whether a trainee program is needed. Resources and support for the program will need to come from top management, and the cooperation of all organizational members involved with the trainees will be essential towards their successful training. Be certain that the need for trainees is supported by organizational members for employment or succession purposes.

Careful Assessment

Ensure that the selection of trainees includes a careful assessment of the applicants' motivational profile. Highly talented people willing to learn and being patient to explore possible job placements make better trainees than candidates who are impatient to settle into one job and to progress upwards.

S. M. Cheng (✉)
Sydney, Australia
e-mail: DosDontsHR@yahoo.com

© Springer-Verlag Berlin Heidelberg 2015
M. Zeuch (ed.), *Dos and Don'ts in Human Resources Management,*
DOI 10.1007/978-3-662-43553-3_8

Clear Communication

Communicate with trainees and other organizational members about the purpose and objectives of the training, and the desired outcomes of the trainee program. Trainees need assurance that the time they spend in training will lead to good positions with commensurate salaries. Existing employees need reassurance of job security, and equitable rewards and promotional prospects being accorded them as well as the new trainees.

Be Supportive

Support trainers, mentors and supervisors who are directly working with the trainees to prepare them for suitable eventual placements. Financial, time and material support may have to be mobilized to enable these individuals to feel appreciated and confident to share expertise and experience with their potential successors.

Monitor Systematically

Monitor systematically the progress of the training, and be honest in conveying the assessment of the trainees. Enable them to make informed decisions about whether to continue with the program, or to quit. Introduce interim achievement milestones and recognize trainees who achieve them so as to motivate them to stay the course. Build exit clauses into the agreement so that either the employer or the trainee can terminate the training at mutually agreed times, without disrupting the work of the unit to which the trainee is attached.

Consider Replacing the On-Job Probation with Trainee Program

Consider the trainee program as the screening mechanism for all new recruits before placement in a permanent position. This can replace the on-job probation where a new recruit may be left to swim or sink without systematic training.

Do not Over-promise

Don't create a hype around the trainee program or its participants such as to give them unreasonably high expectations or feelings of entitlement. Similarly, do not over-promise on what awaits the trainees at the end of training.

Don't Ignore the Interests of Existing Employees

Don't ignore the interests of existing employees who may perceive their positions as being threatened by trainees who are being groomed to replace them.

Don't Allow Mentees to Lose Their Mentors Abruptly

Don't allow mentees to lose their mentors abruptly, as in the case of mentors moving away or leaving the program suddenly. Team mentoring and training in a program will minimize this risk.

Follow Through to the End, and Beyond

Don't launch a trainee program with a lot of hype but fail to check in periodically to demonstrate continuing organizational support for all involved in the program. Follow through to the end, and beyond. An alumni association may be established to enable trainees who have graduated to network and give mutual support as they settle into their regular jobs.

Vocational Training

Rainer Wieland

Ensure Cooperation and Alignment Between Companies and Schools

A major success factor in vocational training is that a school and company work together hand-in-hand to create a consistent learning experience. It is only with this close cooperation that optimal preparation for a job assignment is ensured. Often, several companies work together with a school to reduce one-time costs and share resources.

Invest in Education of Teachers

Teachers at schools do not necessarily have the practical experience which is needed to prepare students for the real-life challenges in their future jobs. This is why companies participating in vocational training should invest in the education and practical experience of teachers, e.g. by inviting them to workshops or by having their own staff train teachers. Therefore good communication- and cooperation skills are needed for all involved partners. To make it perfect, teacher exchanges between different countries are the best way to learn from each other.

R. Wieland (✉)
Gaggenau, Germany
e-mail: DosDontsHR@yahoo.com

© Springer-Verlag Berlin Heidelberg 2015
M. Zeuch (ed.), *Dos and Don'ts in Human Resources Management*,
DOI 10.1007/978-3-662-43553-3_9

Don't Exceed Demand

One of the most important factors in the future attractiveness of a vocational training program is the percentage of participants who find a job within the company after the program. This rate should be close to 100% (at least for those who want to get a job in the company). Graduates not finding a job can only be avoided with sound and rather conservative planning of the volume of new hires needed after the vocational training program finishes.

Don't Use Apprentices as Cheap Workforce

Working and learning must be in line with government and school's regulation. The internship in the third year should give apprentices the opportunity to execute in real situations, what they already learned at school. A mature and qualified supervisor should give feedback after performances. Assignments have to be relevant learning experiences, not just filling capacity gaps!

Take Care of the Participants

Participants in vocational training are typically younger than average new hires. This is why personal guidance is of particular importance to them, which also includes introducing them to professional behavior, business discipline, quality orientation and team work.

Drive Participants' Engagement

For example: Organize a factory tour/office tour at the start of the education, set up a scholarship for excellent performance.

Blue Collar: Pay for Working Clothes for Better Branding

Especially in fast growing markets, an intensive bonding is necessary as graduates of the program are not only needed by your company! Avoid that you "educate for competitors"! For example, providing special working clothes with your company logo, enhances a feeling of belonging and hence retention.

Implement New Teaching Methods

While face to face training is still the major method, new forms of teaching (e.g. eLearning, action-based learning, and team assignments) should gradually be implemented. Teachers and apprentices need time to get familiar with these new teaching methods.

Executive Search

Lorenz Illing

Be Aware of the Magnitude of Hiring the Right or Wrong Executive

Regardless of industry, business model and company size, having the right executives and leaders on your management team is probably one of the most important competitive advantages you have to fight for. Outstanding executives and leaders are those who shape companies culture and direction, leverage companies resources to the edge and adopt disruptive innovations fast in order to roll past the competition.

Imagining the consequences and costs of not having the right executives in charge, the value created through a good executive search consultancy becomes quite perceptible.

Decide on a Partner—Not on a Service Provider

By selecting an executive search consultancy you decide on not only a simple service provider but a partner, which will ideally stay at your side as a consultant for many years. The more the consultancy knows about you and your business, the better it can provide its service of finding the best executives and experts fitting to your unique wants and needs.

L. Illing (✉)
Berlin, Germany
e-mail: DosDontsHR@yahoo.com

© Springer-Verlag Berlin Heidelberg 2015
M. Zeuch (ed.), *Dos and Don'ts in Human Resources Management*,
DOI 10.1007/978-3-662-43553-3_10

Besides the experience with the vacant profile of yours and the deep knowledge about your specific business and market characteristics, the consultancy also has to be able to master the complexity and holism of the provided executive search process. Now having shortlisted the best consultancies on basis of their professional skills and experiance, choose the one you trust and can build up a long-term partnership with.

Carefully Decide on a Fee Structure

Recruiting firms are paid either on the basis of a successful outcome (i.e. you hire the person suggested by the recruiting firm), on the basis of their efforts (e.g. in hours or days) or a mixture of both (i.e. you pay a fixed fee for the search process and a provision in case of a successful placement). Advantage of the success-based model is that it lowers the financial risk of the client company to a minimum. Hence the financial risk stays at the recruiting firm, which as a consequence can lead to diminishing the most resource- and labor-intense activities and shifting the concentration on a time-driven rather than a quality-driven search process.

Don't Only Focus on Cost

Cost considerations should not play the major role in the discussion about the right recruiting consultancy. Much more important is to identify the recruiting firm, which is most likely able to identify, convince and finally place the best fitting executive. Choosing an economic consultancy might sound financially attractive in the first place but a wrong or sub-optimal executive placement can have a negative impact which exceeds by far the hiring cost due to lost performance, cost of re-hiring and confusion/disorientation of employees regarding the direction of the company.

Don't Forfeit Your Image at Your Candidates

Some executives search firms offer their service on a hundred percent success base so some clients tend to assign several search firms with this fee structure at the same time for the same vacancy. The client's financial risk stays at the same low level because only the successful serach firm needs to be recompensated. Additionally the speed of the search and the quantity of candidates is expected to increase because not only one but several search firms are actively scanning the market. Nevertheless, the possible downside is to forfeit the companies image at the most wanted candidates. Being approached from different executive search agencies for the same position might make the employer appear unorganized, unprofessional or too desperate.

Selection Methods

Carla K. Shull

Tailor the Selection System to the Competencies Required for the Job

A job analysis is conducted to determine what the most important competencies are and what level of proficiency is required for each competency. This provides the foundation for what your selection methods should measure.

Use a Holistic Approach

There are a variety of selection methods and it is important to understand which are better at measuring different characteristics and to combine the methods wisely. For example, cognitive ability is easier to measure using an online test while interpersonal presence would be easier to measure in a face-to-face interview.

Train Selection System Users

Depending on the selection methods that are used, the level of training needed will vary. Some online tests are very easy to interpret so would require little training, while interviews and assessment centers require more rigorous training. System

C. K. Shull (✉)
Denver, CO, USA
e-mail: DosDontsHR@yahoo.com

© Springer-Verlag Berlin Heidelberg 2015
M. Zeuch (ed.), *Dos and Don'ts in Human Resources Management*,
DOI 10.1007/978-3-662-43553-3_11

users should be trained so that consistent approaches and selection criteria are applied across all candidates.

Develop an Efficient Process

If there is a large candidate pool for a position, the selection funnel should start with a method that is easy to administer and screens out unqualified candidates (e.g., online assessment that is relevant to the job). More expensive and labor-intensive methods (e.g., interviews, assessment centers) should be used later in the process once the number of candidates has been reduced.

Consider the Experience of the Candidate

Throughout the selection process, candidates are gathering information about the organization and job to help them make a decision if they receive a job offer. The design of the selection process should allow ample opportunity for the candidate to ask questions, gain a clear understanding of the job, meet people whom they will be working with and for, and obtain information about the culture of the organization.

Evaluate the System

The selection system needs to be monitored and continuously evaluated for ease of administration, legal defensibility, impact on the image or reputation of the organization, validity and cost-effectiveness. Ensure that you have a process that delivers the best possible filtering within the budget available. Also, be able to show the benefits of using your system. If your selection system is effective, benefits can be numerous, including reduced turnover, better culture fit, accelerated productivity of new hires, improved employee performance and better business results.

Keep Your Methods Up-to-Date

Research on selection methods continues to be conducted and it is important to stay abreast of the latest developments. Maintaining current knowledge of the research will help ensure your system is improved when needed.

Be Consistent

The selection methods and processes should be applied consistently across all candidates.

Do Not Use Information Not Relevant to the Job

Use of non-job related information (e.g., gender, minority status, age, medical conditions) may result in discrimination of candidates and lead to legal trouble for the organization.

Do Not Be Too Narrowly Focused

The selection process should measure several job-related competencies. If an organization relies on only one selection method (e.g., just an interview) or on only a few competencies, there will be limited information on the candidate and it will be difficult to determine if they are a good fit for the job or with the organization.

Do Not Build Too Much Redundancy into System

Administration of selection methods often requires a significant amount of time from candidates, recruiters and hiring managers. Ensure that the process is efficient and does not include multiple measures of one characteristic (e.g., cognitive ability assessed with three or four instruments). Also, avoid creating overlap in questions that are asked by interviewers.

Part II
Training and Qualification

Introduction

Matthias Zeuch

Training and qualification enhance the skills and knowledge of employees relevant to their current or future positions.

The classical form of enhancing skills is classroom training with a teacher (trainer) in front of a group of learners.

While this form of training is still predominant, other forms of training have been developed in companies over recent decades, such as:

- self-studies with learning media, computer-based training, audio-books, video etc.
- experience-based learning simulation games, outdoor exercises
- learning projects
- blends of different learning methods

M. Zeuch (✉)
Beijing, China
e-mail: DosDontsHR@yahoo.com

© Springer-Verlag Berlin Heidelberg 2015
M. Zeuch (ed.), *Dos and Don'ts in Human Resources Management*,
DOI 10.1007/978-3-662-43553-3_12

Skill Management

Sandy Chen

Create the Job Description

Skill management's basis is Job Description (JD). Make sure all jobs have a complete job description which specifies all the Key Result Areas (KRA) the job holder is required to deliver.

Develop Skill Profile Based on JD

Analyze what are the necessary skills a job holder needs to have in order to deliver the KRA. Skill profiles should also differentiate between different levels of skills (e.g. "Basic", "Advanced", "Mastery").

Analyze Skill Gaps

While skill profiles represent the demand side, the real skills of job holder represent the supply side. Comparing demanded skills and the real skills of the job holder within the job family leads to the "Skill Gap".

S. Chen (✉)
Shenzhen, China
e-mail: DosDontsHR@yahoo.com

© Springer-Verlag Berlin Heidelberg 2015
M. Zeuch (ed.), *Dos and Don'ts in Human Resources Management,*
DOI 10.1007/978-3-662-43553-3_13

Build on Existing Basis

If, for example, in Compensation and Benefits or Talent Development there already exists a job family model, it is highly advisable to use the same model for defining skill profiles for these job families.

Discuss Certification

Define skill demands via skill profiles and then provide the appropriate learning solution to bring up the job holder's skill up to the required level. An even stronger approach is to test if the employee *really* acquired the skills (as opposed to just attending the class!). Such a "Certification" obviously requires more administrative work, but pays off in terms of the higher effectiveness of the overall skill development process in the company.

Avoid Inflation of Skill Demands

When developing skill profiles in cooperation with experts on the subject matter from the respective departments, there is a risk that skill demands are exaggerated. The reason for this is that people are usually proud of what they are doing and tend to over-emphasize the difficulty of the job and hence the skill requirement. With all due respect to the subject matter experts who help HR by creating skill profiles, HR should try to avoid such inflationary tendencies in the discussion with subject matter experts. We highly recommend that all skills should be derived from the KRA, otherwise it will not be considered.

Avoid Inflation of Job Families and Skill Types

Similar to the first point, the degree of differentiation between job families and skill types has to be managed by HR. Subject matter experts like to differentiate, because they know all the details. Still, HR should try to keep the number of job families and skill categories low. As always, a good constructive dialogue is advisable, exchanging the pros and cons of differentiation.

Training Management

Karen Hughey

Training Quality Management

Ensure that the intended skill transfer really happens and that delivery methods and the organizational conditions are professional. A major information source for this is the collection of feedback from participants and from their supervisors.

Ask for Updates

Even if for capacity reasons you are forced to use the catalogue-based method of training planning, open a channel for the department to express additional training needs which are not covered by the catalogue.

Demand Flexibility from Vendors

One of the challenges in planning training is that external training vendors want to create their plan for the next year early to ensure that their capacities will be optimally used. This goal can interfere with the company's training planning which usually is done after the performance appraisals (or in parallel to them).

K. Hughey (✉)
Overland Park, KS, USA
e-mail: DosDontsHR@yahoo.com

© Springer-Verlag Berlin Heidelberg 2015
M. Zeuch (ed.), *Dos and Don'ts in Human Resources Management*,
DOI 10.1007/978-3-662-43553-3_14

In order to accommodate the vendor's planning, training departments at times feel compelled to book classes prior to having the new data from training planning. This bears the risk that bookings have been done (and paid for) without the corresponding demand. In such cases, the training department starts sending out messages such as, "seats Still free. Please enroll!" which sends the wrong message. The message should be: "Attend training that helps you perform!", even though the message actually is: "Attend training because there are open seats!"

The better strategy is to negotiate hard with training vendors and demand more flexibility from them.

Don't Offer "Nice To Have" Classes

Training should not be mixed up with social clubs or comparable hobby circles. Just because people like a class, does not mean that it has to be offered.

While social clubs can have a justification from an engagement and retention perspective (please refer to Chap. 4), training classes should be offered with the purpose of performance enhancement. Otherwise the training department loses its reputation as a business function.

Conduct Periodic "Temperature Checks"

In dynamic organizations, periodic "temperature checks" need to be scheduled during the year. Quarterly is a good time to have a business strategy review with key leadership in all departments. The purpose of the temperature checks is to review the current performance enhancement training schedule and identify new business needs that may not have been identified due to changing business needs or goals. These new needs must be accommodated and alternative plans put into place to meet the needs. The training department cannot run the risk of alienating itself from business partners by being inflexible to alter training plans as needed.

Keep it Simple

Design a simple training request and delivery process. Internal Business partners do not have time to become bogged down in complicated training request processes. A complicate and inflexible process will result in the training department being viewed as an obstacle to training performance improvement rather than a performance improvement partner.

New Hire Integration

Matthias Zeuch

Start Early

The integration process can even start prior to the first day of work if the company sends to the future employee a welcome package or a special email with company information.

Many companies invite all new recruits, during their first days or weeks of employment, to a "New Hire Day". This day usually includes a mix of information and cultural elements, such as a round of questions and answers with a top executive and/or team development exercises.

Use Peer Mentorships

A proven method of new hire integration is peer mentorships. A peer mentor is a person in a similar job position who already has some job experience. A peer mentor will be assigned to a new hire for the first months to provide guidance, information and answer questions. Peer mentors can significantly support a new hire's emotional integration because the new hire might ask him/her questions which he/she does not want to discuss with the supervisor.

M. Zeuch (✉)
Beijing, China
e-mail: DosDontsHR@yahoo.com

© Springer-Verlag Berlin Heidelberg 2015
M. Zeuch (ed.), *Dos and Don'ts in Human Resources Management*,
DOI 10.1007/978-3-662-43553-3_15

Use Different Methods

- Special new hire integration online forum.
- Guideline for supervisors about the dos and don'ts regarding new hires.
- Operational checklist for new hire integration. (IT set-up, workspace set-up, medical check, company badge, cell phone, keys …)
- On-boarding discussion with HR.
- "Tea with the President" or "Fireside Chat" for a smaller group of new hires with the CEO.

Plan with Top Executives Well in Advance

If you plan to involve top executives in your new hire integration program, schedule with them well in advance and also prepare for back-up in case of cancellations due to other urgent business needs.

Think About Symbolic Experiences

The first days in the company have a major, long-term influence on the spirit of the employee. Think about ways to create a positive symbolic activity that the new hires will remember.

Leadership Training

John van Dijk

Target All (Potential) Leaders

Traditionally, leadership training focused on middle- and top management. In recent years, the selection and training of entry level leaders gained more attention, because this specifically targets people who, for the first time in their careers, are going to take over formal leadership responsibilities. Furthermore it enlarges your chances for discovering talent within the company and fills your leadership pipeline.

Mix with Experiential Learning

Leadership training should be a mix of trainer input and experience-based learning, helping participants to gain an understanding of what it means to lead themselves, other people and organizations in daily practice and to acquire knowledge about and develop skills in major leadership instruments (e.g. planning, organizing, communicating, decision making, motivating).

J. van Dijk (✉)
Mandaluyong City, Philippines
e-mail: DosDontsHR@yahoo.com

© Springer-Verlag Berlin Heidelberg 2015
M. Zeuch (ed.), *Dos and Don'ts in Human Resources Management*,
DOI 10.1007/978-3-662-43553-3_16

47

Consider New Developments

Leadership training should address the changes in the corporate landscape and organization. Examples are:

- Globalization and Intercultural Leadership.
- Increasing Emphasis on Sustainability.
- Leading Virtual Teams.
- Leading in the Matrix.
- Leading without Hierarchical Power (e.g. for project managers).
- Leading Change.

Do Start with Entry Level Leadership

As already mentioned, entry level leaders, for the first time in their careers, take over leadership responsibilities. It is one of the major lessons for this target group, that even though they personally might feel unchanged, their team members see them differently now. They have expectations towards the new leader, they observe/interpret/comment on their new leader. Entry level leadership training deals with this role change.

Do Prefer Several Modules

As opposed to many other training topics which can be taught in 1 or 2 days, learning leadership is a development process over time. Bear in mind the sequence: Lead Yourself, Lead Others, Lead an Organization. It is highly advisable to have a group of (future) leaders go through a sequence of training experiences together, always over several months, in order to reflect and apply what has been learned during the module. Such groups will develop mutual trust which is necessary to share uncertainties and concerns regarding their own leadership role.

Don't Engage Trainers Who Preach

Charismatic leadership trainers who "preach" about leadership are entertaining and often have good points about certain specific aspects of leadership behavior. The effect of such training courses, however, is limited because the topics are not transferred into the participants' real-life environment.

In order to be effective, leadership training has to break down the barrier between classroom and work, bring in real-life examples of the participants and help them take their lessons learned back into their work environment. This requires trainers who have a comprehensive view on leadership, practice "active listening" and are much differentiated when they give advice.

New Learning Methods

Laurence Baltzer

New Learning methods have grown far beyond eLearning. Combinations of phone and video conferencing, synchronous and asynchronous work on dedicated learning platforms, the usage of virtual worlds will become more and more the new reality of learning.

Blend of Methods

New Learning methods can be used as a stand-alone method or in combination with other methods such as classical classroom learning or project assignments ("blended learning").

Long Term Learning Community

As opposed to the typical classroom training, new learning methods give the opportunity to spread the learning over a few months, which divides the learning into digestible bits and gives the chance to reflect learnings with the peer group. Transfer of learning in "real life" becomes part of the training, development of new skills becomes sustainable and networking is enhanced.

L. Baltzer (✉)
Berlin, Germany
e-mail: DosDontsHR@yahoo.com

© Springer-Verlag Berlin Heidelberg 2015
M. Zeuch (ed.), *Dos and Don'ts in Human Resources Management,*
DOI 10.1007/978-3-662-43553-3_17

Applications

One typical application of new learning methods is to bring together a group of learners with different levels of knowledge virtually (Phone, Video conference, Virtual World), before the classroom training starts. Here they can already get to know each other and do some preparational work. This enhances the effectiveness of the cost-intensive classroom training.

Similarly, virtual learning after classroom training will give the opportunity to review the learnings as well as the practice. It will allow for peer consulting and create a strong and potentially long lasting network amongst the participants.

Even in a complete virtual training with no face-to-face element, it is possible to create a feeling of belonging and closeness and to work intensively on topics like behaviour and leadership.

Seize the Possibilities

Obviously, information technology opens new, exciting ways of communication, which can and should be used for training as well. Particularly younger generations entering the corporate world will demand training, which matches their style. New Learning methods include synchroneous and asynchroneous elements, which allow for much more flexibility in terms of when and how participants will be focusing on learning.

Do Not Rely on "Classical Facilitation Methods" Only

As "hiding" is easier in the virtual world than in a classroom training, it is essential to create a feeling of belonging to the participant group and to involve the participants over and over again. This asks for a different facilitation than the classroom training facilitation and is a critical success factor for the success of your training. One important factor for a lively training group is the group size: in order to have all participants actively involved, you should restrict the group to 12 participants.

Team Development

Matthias Zeuch

Find the Right Triggers

Some departments do team development frequently without any particular initiating situation in order to further enhance cooperation and effectiveness of the team. In other cases, there is a special initiating reason ("trigger") for conducting the team development.

Typical triggers of team development are:

- Two former separated team become one team.
- Destructive competition between team members.
- Economic crisis/ need for significant cost cuts.
- Significant changes in the leadership of the team.
- Internationalization of the company requires teams to collaborate across borders.
- Project kick-off or closing/debrief.

M. Zeuch (✉)
Beijing, China

© Springer-Verlag Berlin Heidelberg 2015
M. Zeuch (ed.), *Dos and Don'ts in Human Resources Management,*
DOI 10.1007/978-3-662-43553-3_18

Include All

When doing team development exercises, do not select an activity that excludes people.

E.g.: Skiing trips might be great for those who like skiing, but not really exciting for those who feel uncomfortable comfortable with skiing. As head of a department remember, if you like something, not everybody else might be as excited as you about it.

Get Professional Support

Either within the HR/Training department there are experienced people who can develop, facilitate and de-brief team development events or your get external support from companies specializing in this. The more unusual the exercise is and the more it takes the team out of its comfort-zone, the more it is advisable to have facilitators who do not do this for the first time!

Select Location Carefully

In general, as organizer or leader of the meeting, you should know the location or have a person you trust and who knows the location.

Examples:

- Many hotels have their meeting rooms in the basement without windows, this can turn the most optimistic team into collective depression …
- Check other events take place at the same location and if this is what you want.
- Ideally there should be opportunities to spend breaks outside (unless the whole event is anyway outdoors).
- In case of events for more than 1 day, make sure that there is a convenient and attractive place to spend the evening together with the team. Rather make reservations in advance.
- Do prefer buffet-style food for lunch to avoid unwanted delays due to service shortage in the hotel.

Do Not Rush

Do not rush through exercises like you usually rush through the agenda of your business meetings. Team development events live very much from the times in-between the exercises, the reflections and the exchange between people.

Do Not Under-estimate Organizational Effort

To avoid last-minute stress, start early with preparation. There is hardly any event in which things run 100 % according to plan. You always need a plan B, e.g. for an outdoor event in case the weather is not favorable.

Part III
Performance and Talent

Introduction

Nora Binder

Multiple factors determine the competitive advantage of a company: financial capital, innovations, and technologies; but there is only one sustained and not easily replicated one: talent and how it is managed. Activities in this area have the goal of always having the right people in the right positions: today, tomorrow and in the long-term.

Not only people with talent for upper management are "talents." Talents are engaged, high performing people who add significant value to a company, as diligent experts in accounting, as creative minds in innovation centers or as entrepreneurial and inspiring leaders in upper management positions. Talent development focuses on the individual and his or her career progression within the company.

Talent development has the perspective of "looking back" at past performance and "looking forward" to future assignments. To achieve this, a talent management plan needs to be closely aligned with the company's strategic goals and business needs—goal alignment clarifies job roles and demonstrates ongoing values of the employee to the organization. By creating employee ownership in the company's success and high employee commitment, talents are supported to reach the desired high levels of job performance.

N. Binder (✉)
Vienna, Austria
e-mail: DosDontsHR@yahoo.com

© Springer-Verlag Berlin Heidelberg 2015
M. Zeuch (ed.), *Dos and Don'ts in Human Resources Management,*
DOI 10.1007/978-3-662-43553-3_19

Performance and Potential Management

Rainer Allinger, Pirkko Erichsen and Kerstin Beckers

Create Acceptance and Commitment to Your Assessment

Make sure the assessment tools and results have top management attention. Ensure the assessors are well selected and highly respected. Ensure the assessment results are respected.

Ensure Transparency and Objectivity in Your Assessment

Assessment criteria and assessment pocess have to be transparent. Ensure appraisal input from at least one additional source beside supervisor's appraisal (e.g. additional appraisal from selected executive; integration of appraisal within supervisors peer group; assessment center).

R. Allinger (✉) · K. Beckers
Berlin, Germany
e-mail: DosDontsHR@yahoo.com

P. Erichsen
Stuttgart, Germany

© Springer-Verlag Berlin Heidelberg 2015
M. Zeuch (ed.), *Dos and Don'ts in Human Resources Management*,
DOI 10.1007/978-3-662-43553-3_20

No Work-Around

Do not allow work-around of your policy regarding performance and potential management. If certain aspects of your policy are not feasible, change the policy rather than tolerating non-compliance with your required standards.

Ensure Global Standard

In international organizations: ensure that you have a good overview of performance and potential in your country organizations. Ensure a global standard of assessment criteria to enable international development of talent.

SMART Target

Set targets which are Specific, Measurable, Achievable, Realistic and Timely.

Do Not Forget Qualitative Targets

Integrate Leadership behavior in target agreement and/or evaluation of target achievement.

Combine Your Performance Management System with Measuring Values and Behavior

Ensure as an organization that you also track how targets are achieved to enhance a mindset defined by the company's values.

Positive and outstanding behavior according to your set of behaviors should be encouraged and vice versa behavior you would not like to embed in your organization should be fed back.

Require Leaders to Give Feedback

Make feedback to employees about their performance assessment and development discussions regarding their potential assessment mandatory.

Avoid Surprises

The final performance rating at year end should not come as a surprise! To prevent surprises and give clear guidance, supervisors should give frequent feedback throughout the year, and HR should encourage them to do so. Potentially, HR should implement a formal mid-year review.

Do Not Only Think Vertically

Ensure that a horizontal potential statement is considered as well as an important development opportunity.

Enrich Your Potential Statement

Link a concrete developmental initiative (focusing on areas where the assessment indicates development needs) to your potential statement.

Activate Employees

Encourage employees to play an active role in their career planning and career development.

Do Not Underestimate Expectations

Every potential statement creates expectations. Make sure, that they are/become realistic.

Development Discussions and Plans

Agnes Tse

As Supervisor Providing Feedback

Prepare Yourself

Reserve enough time with the employee and schedule well in advance to allow for in-depth preparation by yourself and the employee.

Ask, Don't Tell

Feedback is much more effective if you can get employees to see for themselves what is good in their performance.

Describe, Don't Judge

Feedback is not the same as criticism; feedback should be neutral and not judgmental. Describe what the case is and let the employees draw their own conclusions; in particular in case of negative messages: not "you are lazy" but "during the last weeks I observed less output from you than before".

A. Tse (✉)
Shanghai, China
e-mail: DosDontsHR@yahoo.com

© Springer-Verlag Berlin Heidelberg 2015
M. Zeuch (ed.), *Dos and Don'ts in Human Resources Management*,
DOI 10.1007/978-3-662-43553-3_21

Behaviour, Not Personality

Feedback can soon turn personal; stick to commenting on what employees do instead of what kind of people they are.

Be Specific

Don't just say you like or don't like a person's work or behaviour; make it clear and specific; being descriptive will make it easier for employees to make use of your feedback.

Be Constructive

Don't use feedback as an excuse to get something off your chest; avoid negative messages if something is wrong and discuss constructive ways to make it better; be clear about consequences; end your feedback on a positive note.

Constant Feedback

Do not limit feedback to one yearly development discussion, but use "coachable moments" such as a joint car ride after a customer meeting for this.

Follow-Up

Document the result of the discussion as a development plan in written form. When formulating the plan, the actions should be **SMART** (compare to "Performance and Potential Management).

As Supervisor, Mind the Difference

Do not forget that employees might have different career (and life) plans than you think they should have. Particularly, Generation Y people are not automatically geared towards a career climbing the corporate ladder! Your role is to provide guidance and resources to support their development.

As Employee, When Receiving Feedback

Prepare Yourself for the Discussion

Ask yourself what your real goals are and how your supervisor can support you in these.

Be Open, Not Defensive

See feedback as a useful opportunity to learn how your behaviour has come over to other people or affected them; do not spend time on defending and justification; remember that "perception is reality"; decide on your own which feedback should change your behavior and which not.

Listen and Clarify

Don't interrupt when someone is giving you feedback; listen actively and make sure you fully understand what is being said before responding; ask questions to clarify, if necessary.

Seek Specific Suggestions to Improve

Discuss with the supervisor who gives you feedback what you might do differently to improve your performance; if you do make changes, ask feedback on the results.

As Employee, You Are in Charge

Do not expect the supervisor or the company to take care of your development plan and its follow-up. Do understand it as your own task, supported by your supervisor and the company. Remember—No Pain; No Gain!

Talent Development Groups

Matthias Zeuch

Consider Pros and Cons

Before implementing a talent development group, evaluate carefully the pros and cons of such a group. Balance the need for special attention for high potentials versus the signal to those who do not belong to the group.

Limit the Size of the Group

You will need top management attention and support (ideally mentorships from top managers to participants of the group). Their capacity for mentorship and other forms of attention to group members has limits, due to the nature of their roles in the organization.

Involve Top Management

Involve top management in the design and selection process of the group. Ensure their commitment to supporting the group prior to implementation.

M. Zeuch (✉)
Beijing, China
e-mail: DosDontsHR@yahoo.com

© Springer-Verlag Berlin Heidelberg 2015
M. Zeuch (ed.), *Dos and Don'ts in Human Resources Management*,
DOI 10.1007/978-3-662-43553-3_22

Manage Expectations

Communicate to the participants that being part of the group provides an *opportunity but no automatism* for further career development. Do not create overly high expectations about career development in employees joining the group. This starts when creating a name for the group (e.g. a name like "Fast Track" will clearly create expectations which you might not be able to fulfill).

Track Turnover

Track turnover of the participants of the group. Turnover should be significantly lower than average for comparable peers.

Transparent Selection Criteria

Base the selection process for the group on your existing performance and potential management, and make criteria transparent to indicate equal opportunities for all employees in the selection process.

Don't Forget about the Graduates

Do not forget to take care of graduates from the program. There is a risk that, after the program comes to an end, they feel a lack of attention, which can cause a higher risk of turnover.

Don't Forget about the Others

Do not forget about other talented employees. Balance HR attention and top management attention for group members and non-group members.

International Talent Development

Sylke Piéch

In growth markets there is a need to empower local talent and develop this to take on high-level positions. Otherwise, the company will not be able to attract and retain talent in the market, because talented local people do not see sufficient development perspective for themselves ("glass ceiling"). To summarize, international talent development means both globalization and localization of talent.

Nurture Development

A company is only as good as its employees. Their potential is the company's best asset. It is vital to understand and nurture the development of this asset. This includes important factors such as motivation, efficiency, skill development and lifelong learning. People's self-esteem grows when their talent flourishes.

Talent Internationalization

Select candidates for international assignments based on their technical skills and experience as well as their intercultural competence. Being successful in one's home environment does not guarantee success abroad. In particular, having respect for people with different backgrounds or values, active listening skills, a keen in-

S. Piéch (✉)
Berlin, Germany
e-mail: DosDontsHR@yahoo.com

© Springer-Verlag Berlin Heidelberg 2015
M. Zeuch (ed.), *Dos and Don'ts in Human Resources Management*,
DOI 10.1007/978-3-662-43553-3_23

terest in other cultures and the ability to deal with uncertainty are key "soft" criteria to be considered during selection in order to avoid a "hard landing" abroad.

Invest in Training

Invest in intercultural training and language coaching for employees and their families prior to sending them abroad.

Plan Repatriation in Advance

Ensure clarity about future development (repatriation or further international development) for the employee well before the assignment is scheduled to end; otherwise, there is a risk of losing a valuable employee, which the company has invested in, due to the international assignment.

Talent Localization

In growth markets such as Brazil, Russia, India and China ("BRIC countries"):

- Apply the company's performance and potential management process in growth markets at least as intensively as in other markets.
- Identify local talent for higher level positions or more complex challenges early on and help prepare them with clear development plans and programs. Make rotations to your home markets a part of such plans and programs.
- Consider hiring some external middle and/or top management locally to quickly increase the share of locals in your management team.
- Set targets for the share of local talent in your management team in growth markets and track achievement regularly.

Don't Forget Families

Encourage employees to involve their family in the decision-making process regarding the international assignment. It has been shown that the international assignee often has less intercultural challenges to solve than their trailing spouse, who has to deal with schools, kindergarten, craftsmen, utility providers and other "real-life" challenges in the foreign country. When discussing international assignments with employees, spouses should be involved early on in the conversation and special consideration should be made for children. The success of the assignment is endangered if the family is negatively affected during this time.

Don't Make Intercultural Competence Optional

Intercultural competence is just as important as technical skills, if not more so, to ensure the success of an international assignment. Expertise and knowledge will not help the international assignee if they are not able to operate effectively in the host country. Keep in mind that success in one's home environment does not guarantee success abroad. Particularly, having respect for people with different backgrounds or values, active listening skills, a keen interest in other cultures and the ability to deal with uncertainty are key "soft" criteria to be considered during selection in order to avoid a "hard landing" abroad.

Coaching

Matthias Zeuch

Coaching Starts with Listening

A coach supports his/her coachee (person who is coached) in becoming successful. To do so, the coach actively listens to the motivations, goals and emotions of the coachee, develops an understanding of the coachee's relevant environment and jointly develops strategies with the coachee for his/her success. This also includes an understanding of what "success" means for the coachee.

Coaches Are Independent

A true coach does not have any personal stake in the environment of the coachee and hence is independent. This is why the concept of "leader as coach" has its limits, because the leader has self-interest, which might differ and even be in conflict with the coachee's interests. Certainly, a "coaching leadership style" is desirable in which a leader displays behaviors, such as active listening and a supportive attitude towards the employee.

M. Zeuch (✉)
Beijing, China
e-mail: DosDontsHR@yahoo.com

© Springer-Verlag Berlin Heidelberg 2015
M. Zeuch (ed.), *Dos and Don'ts in Human Resources Management,*
DOI 10.1007/978-3-662-43553-3_24

Select Coaches Carefully

The expertise for real coaching clearly is similar to psychotherapy even though a coaching may not silently turn into a psychotherapy. A coach has to know where the limits of coaching are! Internal experienced staff may become coaches, but only after a structured education and selection/quality management process. Coachees usually develop trust and hence a certain kind of vulnerability towards the coach which the coach has to deal with in a professional and ethically responsible manner. Not everybody can be coach and also not everybody should be coach!

Mentoring

Karen Minor

A Mentor Is Not a Coach

A Mentor provides guidance, shares experience and, at times, also opens doors for the future development of his/her Mentee (person who is mentored). A Mentor often is a high-ranking, experienced staff member of the company. At a minimum, the Mentor should be at least one level higher than the Mentee. A Mentor should also display a "coaching style." However, a Mentor is not an independent coach. The Mentor might, for example, wish to have the Mentee working in his/her department in the future.

Do Define Key Roles in a Mentoring Program

The Mentor is a person who shares their experience to assist a colleague with their career. That colleague is the Mentee, and their role is an active one, they need to be engaged in their own development. Another role is that of the Program Manager. This role is helpful in a company to handle administration, program requirements, and to field questions or concerns.

K. Minor (✉)
West Bloomfield, MI, USA
e-mail: DosDontsHR@yahoo.com

© Springer-Verlag Berlin Heidelberg 2015
M. Zeuch (ed.), *Dos and Don'ts in Human Resources Management*,
DOI 10.1007/978-3-662-43553-3_25

Select the Right Mentors

Do assure that a Mentor is a person with greater experience that the Mentee, and that the Mentor is a person willing and able to provide guidance and share experience. As an initial step, the Mentor should discuss with the Mentee what they want to get out of the mentoring. Don't forget that Mentors need to know what their role is, and how they can be the best resource for the Mentee. Sometimes Mentors do not want to participate because they may not know how they can contribute. They may even be insecure with this role which is out of their comfort zone. Do share tips for the Mentor to help them be the best in this important role. Don't allow Mentors to care more than the Mentee.

Manage Mentees' Expectations

Don't allow Mentees to expect that the Mentor will definitively open doors for a promotion of his/her mentee. This type of advocacy for a Mentee's career needs to be earned by the Mentee, and is truly the highest level of mentoring.

Ensure Confidentiality and Focus

Do assure that both Mentors and Mentee understand that this relationship is confidential, and is a purposeful and focused business relationship. The development needs of the Mentee are the focus.

The Mentees Should Drive the Process

Do be sure that Mentees understand that they drive the mentoring relationship, and that they know how to maximize the relationship with their Mentor. The Mentees should take responsibility for the scheduling of the meetings with their Mentor.

Ensure Commitment of Leadership Team

Do assure that the leadership team believes in Mentoring, and is involved in mentoring. This will set the expectation that mentoring is important to the company.

Ensure Commitment of Mentors and Mentees

Don't assign Mentors or Mentees who are not committed to the program. Don't include Mentors or Mentees in the program if they do not make the time commitment. This can result in frustration for either participant. The Program Manager should set the expectations up front.

Don't Focus on Superstar Mentors

Don't overload the high level, superstar Mentors. You do not want to burn out the "popular" Mentors, and will not give other possible Mentors the opportunity.

Do Have Guidelines and Expected Results

Align guidelines and expectations for the mentoring program with the development objectives of the company. This will help the Mentee and Mentor manage this purposeful business relationship. For example, if the company expects to acquire a subsidiary, there may be the need for leadership skills, knowledge of acquisition and assimilation as well as the technical knowledge.

Consider Different Types of Mentorship Programs

Do educate the participants on the various types of mentoring relationships, and the type of mentoring program in your company. For example, there can be a junior mentoring program that assigns new employees to a tenured employee, with the objective of making the new person feel welcome and to answer questions. There can also be a mentoring program assigning executive Mentors with the expected future executives to work on leadership competencies.

Ensure Matching

Don't leave the matching to chance. Have program objectives for the Mentees, and match them with a Mentor who can best assist with the development.

Set Time Frame for the Program

Don't have a program that is open ended time wise. A 6-months-long program, with check in events managed by the Program Manager is recommended, and a shorter program for more junior team members. Some relationships will continue naturally.

Avoid Favouritism

Don't allow the mentoring relationship to be a source of preferential treatment. Mentors must not overdo their roles by using their power to promote "their" Mentees if they are not the most suitable person.

Succession Planning

Ulrike Hildebrand

Companies Should Be Doing Succession Planning for the Right Reasons

- Risk management
- Talent retention

This is the only way to gain serious commitment to the process. Companies should not do succession planning, because it is the popular thing to do or to keep busy. Doing it without the necessary level of commitment will cause more harm than good.

Ensure Alignment with Business Strategy

The process needs to address workforce planning in the long term and may have to be adjusted on a regular basis accordingly. Define a clear process that fits to the company and its existing processes, and hold people accountable to it. Take time to customize where necessary.

U. Hildebrand (✉)
Chicago, IL, USA
e-mail: DosDontsHR@yahoo.com

© Springer-Verlag Berlin Heidelberg 2015
M. Zeuch (ed.), *Dos and Don'ts in Human Resources Management,*
DOI 10.1007/978-3-662-43553-3_26

Be Clear How Strong the Process Should be

Is it done just to assess the current bench strength or are there internal placement goals to be met? The solution in between could be to make a potential internal successor one candidate that is compared to candidates from the external market.

Take Time to Develop the Leadership Competencies/ Competency Model

That will address future needs of the company. They will also create a more objective base for evaluation. If the definition of competencies is not done or rushed, the identification of candidates will be more subjective and future leadership needs of the company may not be addressed. Implementing an "off the shelf" process without customization will impact the quality of the outcome and the credibility of the process.

Be Clear About Communication

What, when, how and by whom. Be consistent in the communication effort. Being unclear of how the process will be used means the desired outcome is not clear. Without a defined outcome the execution will suffer, and with that increases the possibility of the effort being a waste of time. Lack of or inconsistency in communication creates uncertainty, which will affect morale and productivity.

Manage Expectations of Supervisors and Employees

In regards to their roles and responsibilities in the process, and the outcomes of the process, not managing expectations or not doing so properly will create disappointment and loss of trust—first in the process, then in leadership, then in the company.

Involve Senior Leadership

Ensure senior leadership has bought in and is actively involved and supporting it. Without leadership support and drive, this process is a waste of time.

Ensure Employees Are Actively Involved in Their Own Career Planning and Development

Employee engagement in their own development should be a key factor in placement decisions. Employees that are not taking the initiative and responsibility for their own development are often not the right people for the next level (leadership) role.

The more manual the process, the more time and effort it will require and the more difficult it will be to get the proper level of engagement.

Utilize Technology

If at all possible, utilize technology to reduce time spent and risk of manual errors.

Quality Is Key

The quality of the process defines the quality of the outcome. The desired quality of the outcome is a list of "true" or "real" successors—not just names. Companies should be aware of and avoid the temptation of putting a lot of names down. If quantity (number of names) is higher valued than quality of candidates, it may provide instant gratification at the end of a long calibration meeting, but it will not be satisfying when the identified candidates are either not successful, or not even promoted.

Invest in the Individual Development

When doing succession planning, a company should also invest in the individual development that will be recommended as a result of the process. It is the follow up and follow through on the commitment, and without resources and willingness to invest in individual development, the entire process can at best provide a snapshot of the talent bench at a certain moment in time. Lack of follow up with individual development planning may not only create confusion, but more likely disappointment. The process will not have the desired effect on retention, and of course the succession plan will not evolve over time. If a company decided that they cannot or will not invest in the development of the people, they should probably stick to a "behind closed doors" approach of succession planning.

Motivate Candidates

Ensure that the candidates identified are not only capable, but also motivated to be part of succession planning and related development activities. It is relatively easy to not verify with the candidate—all too often it is assumed that the employee is interested and willing to move up; and sometimes employees will say they are, because they feel it is expected of them. These candidates are less likely to be successful.

Be Clear that Succession Planning Is a Long Term Process

Starting out it may not provide "enough" candidates, but over time (years!) the company will be able to develop its own talent and create a meaningful bench. Do not consider this a one-time project. If not reviewed and adapted on a regular basis, it will lead to an outcome that does not meet business needs. Doing succession planning once or sporadically every so many years will not yield the desired outcome. Patience and perseverance are important, especially for leadership—they need to understand that developing talent takes time.

Part IV
Engagement and Retention

Introduction

Janina Schönebeck and Manfred Schönebeck

Until the 1990s, employee satisfaction was the most commonly used employee opinion research concept. While employee satisfaction can be understood in terms of its relationship with other drivers such as loyalty, commitment/engagement, business performance and many more, sub-concepts of employee satisfaction have gained ground ever since. There are two main sub-concepts that are of tremendous importance and are widely discussed in the literature and companies all over the world—these are "loyalty" and "engagement." Anyhow the differentiation of employee satisfaction, loyalty and engagement is somewhat difficult to be determined since there are varieties of studies that provide more or less similar definitions. Consequential the one cannot precisely be separated from the other. As it is the case for many research areas, trends rise and fall at times appropriate.

Despite the vague distinction, the three concepts have something in common which is the necessity to create additional values for the employee besides simply paying salaries and offering legally required benefits. Employees want to value, enjoy and believe in what they do, which strongly emphasizes that they work for purpose rather than for money.

J. Schönebeck (✉) · M. Schönebeck
Berlin, Germany
e-mail: DosDontsHR@yahoo.com

M. Schönebeck
e-mail: DosDontsHR@yahoo.com

© Springer-Verlag Berlin Heidelberg 2015
M. Zeuch (ed.), *Dos and Don'ts in Human Resources Management*,
DOI 10.1007/978-3-662-43553-3_27

This chapter will emphasize the ideal of an engaged employee and show the relation of increasing employee engagement to employee retention. That is why companies have to develop an in-depth understanding of the needs of their employees, for example, by conducting employee surveys, in order to develop measures matching these needs. The topics introduced in this chapter demonstrate measures that embrace the idea of an employee oriented fulfillment of demands.

Employee Surveys

Janina Schönebeck and Manfred Schönebeck

Frequent and Consistent

In order to see developments in the various areas, employee surveys should be conducted yearly and with the same questions. Updates of the questions or additions should only be made if necessary (e.g. because the company wants to know something about a recent event, recent change, etc.).

Avoid Off-the-rack Questionnaires

Because every company is different, it is not advisable to use the same questionnaires throughout different companies. Only if you have to compare yourself with other companies it is useful, otherwise you should design your own standardized questionnaire in order to receive information about your company specific reality. Only customized questionnaires are able to give you the insights that are necessary to better understand your company.

J. Schönebeck (✉) · M. Schönebeck
Berlin, Germany
e-mail: DosDontsHR@yahoo.com

© Springer-Verlag Berlin Heidelberg 2015
M. Zeuch (ed.), *Dos and Don'ts in Human Resources Management,*
DOI 10.1007/978-3-662-43553-3_28

Keep It Short and Simple

Questions should be easy to understand and avoid ambiguous meanings. Answering the survey should not be a pain for the employees and have an adequate length.

Don't Underestimate Scientifically Substantiated Questionnaires

Scamped questionnaires pave to way to wrong conclusions. Invest time, effort and money into the development of your questionnaire. Because the questionnaire is your ground work and defines the quality of your concluding measurements, it should be reliable and strong. There is not too much effort you can put into its development. The better your questionnaire is designed in the beginning the more reliable results are achieved and the more effective and purposeful measures can be derived.

Don't Forget Hypotheses Postulation

Before starting the measurement you should be aware of your hypotheses otherwise your measurement will show useless results.

Create Acceptance

In order to achieve high participation rates and acceptance for the measurement program, design a tangible communication campaign for your survey. Forcing your measurement program on your employees without aiming for their acceptance and understanding regarding the aim and purpose of the program will entail results that are not necessarily representative and consequentially will not prepare the ground for the right conclusions and actions. You may also consider other measures to achieve a high participation rate, e.g., a publicly displayed "participation cockpit" revealing the participation rates department-by-department and hence raise a competitive spirit. Consider that acceptance among employees often starts with the acceptance of the work council. The support of the work council will make things easier for you.

Be Aware of Relation Between Measurement Results and Management Reaction

When presenting a measurement result, you should always consider the necessary management reaction. If such a relation is ignored, the measurement result will not be of strong value for you. Do not ask questions about potential changes in a certain area and afterwards avoid approaching this area. Decide before you do the survey in which areas you are willing to make amendments.

Don't Forget Communicating Results

One of the biggest mistakes when doing a survey is to stop activities after the survey has been conducted and evaluated. If you have achieved a general acceptance of your measurement program among employees, you have the responsibility to communicate the results. It even is expected. Not fulfilling this responsibility will destroy your employees' trust in your seriousness and reliability. Do not forget thanking your employees for their participation. Furthermore, communicate the actions and changes which have been made based on the valuable survey results.

Don't Be Frustrated by Bad Results

Survey results are not always as we would wish. It is of utmost importance to maintain a thankful attitude towards those who came up with criticism! As long as people share their criticism with you and are honest, even if it seems too extreme in your opinion, you will be able to develop and improve the company by working with all kinds of feedback. Take the chance to include any opinion in your measures to pave the way for a successful and strong future of your company.

Retention Tools

Manfred Schönebeck

Find the Factors Behind Employee and Manager Satisfaction in Your Company by Using Customized Satisfaction Questionnaires

Do your own tailor made research—**Don't** use "off-the-rack" questionnaires. It's not difficult to create your own satisfaction measurement and analyse your data with factor analysis. You need to discover the driving factors behind the behaviour and behind the verbal feedback which is, at most times, a logical concept rather than indistinguishable emotional feedback.

Don't Wake Up Too Late: Be Aware of Your Employees' Plans to Change

Unfortunately employee turnover carries a heave price tag. The biggest damage is of emotional nature—the team feeling is disturbed. Loosing valuable employees is accompanied by unintentional costs, knowledge loss and it deteriorates employee satisfaction rates in the factors "Brand" and "Team." Before you take measures to enhance your retention rate you should become aware of the reasons why people leave. One popular reason most certainly will be "lack of appreciation." You will have to answer the why-question not only to change your employees' minds but also your own behaviour or even your company's culture. You may use exit surveys and interviews to root the cause.

M. Schönebeck (✉)
Berlin, Germany
e-mail: DosDontsHR@yahoo.com

© Springer-Verlag Berlin Heidelberg 2015
M. Zeuch (ed.), *Dos and Don'ts in Human Resources Management*,
DOI 10.1007/978-3-662-43553-3_29

Pivot Retention Relevant Value Propositions

If you want to maintain a competitive advantage as employer of first choice, you should work on your organization's value proposition in terms of retention. Despite your company's specific areas of trouble (your company's specific factors), that should be detected with factor analysis and that need to be addressed in a customized manner, the measures you most likely are going to detect may be assembled under generic themes such as provide a compelling future, opportunities for individual growth, a positive work environment, work-life balance, insurance and financial rewards.

Don't Only Focus on Fundamental Retention Philosophy: Do Also Invest in Dynamic Change Management

Once you are aware of your employees' reasons to change and once you have detected the retention relevant value proposition of your company, you have to strengthen your efforts by articulating a fundamental philosophy guiding your actions and decisions. Only by raising your retention relevant measures into your overall company strategy by fostering a commonly agreed and goal-oriented philosophy you will be able to lend it the importance it will need for a permanent ascertainment and successful change management.

Don't Ask, Who Is Worth the Effort—This Is a Hazardous Question—Do the Best to Empower Team Spirit

Who are the people you want to support? This question soon may lead to the conclusion that not all employees are of equal value for your company and not all of them are worth the effort. This discrimination is dangerous since it creates a culture that is discouraging. It is distinguishing important people who are placed on a pedestal and people that are replaceable and of no value to the company. Retention tools should be provided on all levels and be adapted adequately to serve the needs and expectations of employees in a feasible manner. Remember, there are high performers and high potentials as well as people with scarce and important company knowledge. Don't forget: our basic culture was formed in a family environment and we are highly trained as team players.

Cultural and Social Activities

Olaf B. Tietz

Strengthen Employee Relations

Strengthen the relationship among your employees. A strong communication and cooperation among employees will pave the way to greater team spirit and an efficient and positive working atmosphere. Needed efforts and resources are usually small but have a high impact. Through special games and events you will soon observe genuine improvements. Considering your employee population, you may establish excursions, dinners, sporting activities and games.

Don't Expect Your Employees to Sacrifice Free Time

Because it is of high interest for you to create a more efficient and positive working atmosphere among your employees in order to promote productivity and efficiency to the good of the company, you should understand cultural and social activities as an incentive for your employees rather than asking your employees to sacrifice free time. Your employees will fancy this good gesture and feel valued and appreciated.

Don't Force People into Activities

Do not force people into cultural or social activities. Try to keep participation voluntary. Remember, not all people feel equally comfortable in a social setting. Therefore, you should not put direct or indirect pressure on them to participate.

O. B. Tietz (✉)
Berlin, Germany
e-mail: DosDontsHR@yahoo.com

© Springer-Verlag Berlin Heidelberg 2015
M. Zeuch (ed.), *Dos and Don'ts in Human Resources Management*,
DOI 10.1007/978-3-662-43553-3_30

Discover Positive Effects of Community Initiatives

Build a partnership with an organization in your area. You may consider suggestions of your employees (e.g. kinder garden or nursery school preferably where children of employees are accommodated). If you cooperate with a school you could cater a party for the children of the partner school or organize a joint excursion. The outcome is an improved communication and relationship with the broader community, a challenge and fulfillment for employees to take on responsibilities for the community and an improved company reputation.

Don't Underestimate Impact of Business Partner Relationship

Invite business partners to your company for a special celebration. This is the opportunity to thank your business partners and employees for their successful cooperation. Such event will stimulate the communication among your employees and partners and build strong relationships. You will constitute a philosophy of value and appreciation for each other.

Cooperate with Employee Committees

Consider letting employees decide or co-decide on cultural and social activities. In countries with institutionalized employee representation, it is highly advisable (if not required by law) to work with such committees on the selection of cultural and social activities. Furthermore, the co-creation process creates acceptance among employees and motivates them to participate and believe in its purpose.

Avoid One-Size-Fits-All Approach

International companies face the challenge of intercultural circumstances. If the headquarters decide to foster employee relations, it is advisable to assign or work closely together with national teams who are responsible for the establishment of employee relation programs in the respective country. Allow the countries to design their own ideas that best meet the cultural traits of that country.

Employee Care

Jens Peisert

You Hire a Family

Consider that you don't hire a person in most cases, you hire a family with all problems families have. Include in your employee-benefit-package sensible measures for family-welfare under consideration of life phases.

Seize Important Moments in Employees' Personal Lives

It is of much higher importance to be attentive to these important moments (birthday, child birth, wedding) than provide generous gifts which require (in most countries) taxation. The gestures counts much more than the monetary value.

Health Care Seminars—Kill Two Birds with One Stone

Effective health care seminars can reduce health care costs and be an expression of the company's attention to personal well-being. As a format, established lunch or evening lectures can be used.

J. Peisert (✉)
Berlin, Germany
e-mail: DosDontsHR@yahoo.com

© Springer-Verlag Berlin Heidelberg 2015
M. Zeuch (ed.), *Dos and Don'ts in Human Resources Management*,
DOI 10.1007/978-3-662-43553-3_31

Overly Generous Gifts

Do not use company money for overly generous gifts. This might be seen by investors as a loss of control over finances and might also turn into something negative for employees, if the employee has to bear the taxes for the gift (in some cases, the net value of the gift might be negative for the employee).

Don't Forget People

If you start any of such activities, establish a reminder process so that nobody is forgotten. A positive intention can quickly turn into a de-motivator if such a process lacks equality!

Consider to Pay Special Attention to Top Management and Top Performers

While certain parts of employee care should equally apply to all employees, also consider special programs for those people you want to retain most, for example, your top management and/or your top performers. Concierge programs are one option to enhance work-life balance for these target groups.

Idea Management

Ute Gallmeister

Think Beyond Suggestion Box

Employee suggestion system is a great tool for idea generation, especially in the production sector since generally the value and practicability of an idea can be easily evaluated. But do not limit idea management to an employee suggestion system. Valuable ideas can be generated in all parts of your company.

Create an Open Environment

The generation and identification of good ideas is most promising when the top management is open for new ideas and suggestions. Create a company culture where ideas are welcome. Appreciation of ideas is one of the key factors to employee motivation.

U. Gallmeister (✉)
Berlin, Germany
e-mail: DosDontsHR@yahoo.com

© Springer-Verlag Berlin Heidelberg 2015
M. Zeuch (ed.), *Dos and Don'ts in Human Resources Management,*
DOI 10.1007/978-3-662-43553-3_32

Give Ideas a Chance

Ideas need room to develop. Provide the resources needed. Support ideas wherever possible. Create time slots exclusively for idea development and idea sharing. Consider special formats of idea management, e.g., innovation forums, creative workshops or work groups.

Idea Management Is More than the One Big Idea

Don't wait for the one big idea to pop-up that will solve all your problems. Idea management helps you in many ways. Think about product development, problem solving or process optimization. It does not always have to be the one big idea but various small ones also generate ongoing results and enhancements.

Think Cross-Functionally

Use all of your company's potential for generating ideas. Cross-functional working groups are a great way to do so. You can also include customers or suppliers.

Pursue Your Ideas

Name persons responsible for pursuing ideas and give them resources to do so. Evaluating the value of an idea and making the most of it can be harder than creating it. Many ideas are lost because they are not pursued properly or brought forward to people who benefit from them.

Define a Transparent Policy

In case you use a reward system, it is essential to have clear guidelines describing which ideas qualify for a reward. The higher the job position, the more it is expected that ideas are part of the job description. Usually suggestions regarding people and organizational structures are excluded. Also, be clear upfront on how an award is calculated and if there is a maximum cap on the reward. Remember, ideas do not necessarily have to be compensated monetarily.

Don't Force Ideas

Employee ideas are a valuable asset for your company, but ideas have to come freely. There are employees who generate valuable ideas on a string, while others might not bring up one single good idea. Therefore, be careful to include idea generation into target agreements. Better work with encouragement.

Don't Allow for "Second Salary"

In case you use a monetary reward system, remember that, similar to what was said about employee referral programs; improvement ideas should not become a second job for people, making them reduce effort in their original job duties. Maximum caps of rewards for ideas and a maximum number of eligible ideas per employee per year help to avoid this risk.

Rewards and Recognition

Rainer Schaetzle

Culture Counts More than Financial Value

Basis of any effective recognition culture (regardless what kind of Award programs are set up) are the personal, small and often recognition's expressed in forms like a sincere "thank you!" or a congratulation for a job well done. Maybe accompanied by a card, some small gifts, like a preferred chocolate bar (if the persons like this), a ticket to an event someone is fancy on, and alike. It is not about the financial value—it is about personally taking the time and appreciating what has been done. Recognition programs can be added on this basis in many forms and will complement existing financial driven Rewards programs in a very efficient way.

Make Decision Process and Reasons Transparent

As opposed to normal individual compensation and benefits, the granting of rewards and recognition is often public. Due to this, a fair and transparent decision process is necessary to avoid a feeling of inequity and favoritism amongst employees. As opposed to normal compensation and benefits, companies should consider letting mixed committees (mixed according to diversity categories and position level in company) decide on rewards and recognition.

R. Schaetzle (✉)
Wilen, Switzerland
e-mail: DosDontsHR@yahoo.com

© Springer-Verlag Berlin Heidelberg 2015
M. Zeuch (ed.), *Dos and Don'ts in Human Resources Management*,
DOI 10.1007/978-3-662-43553-3_33

Consider Non-monetary Recognition

Non-monetary recognition can be more effective than monetary recognition. This certainly depends on the type of non-monetary recognition. In a rather hierarchical company, a personal "thank you" from the CEO can have a very strong effect, while in a more collective company, applause from all employees in a town-hall meeting might be more motivating recognition.

Invest in Communication

The announcement and communication about a recognition program should be made in an inspiring, motivating way, not a "We hereby inform you ..." type of way. Even a certain internal branding (logo, catchy name) can be advisable to underline the commitment of the company and the special character of the program.

Hand-over in Public

Use special award ceremonies or embed the hand-over in a town-hall meeting. Communicate the reasons why the employee received the award, ideally linked to your company values and strategy.

Don't Mix with Compensation Tools

Particularly when merits increase budgets are low, rewards and recognition payments can be (mis-)used as set-off for a low merit increase. The problem with such usage of rewards and recognition is that they lose their original intention and uniqueness and become a commodity which will be emotionally difficult to take away in following years. Depending on country's labor laws, repeated payments of such rewards and recognition without special, outstanding reason might even lead to a legal right of employees to receive them also in the future.

Don't Underestimate Workload and Attention

A recognition program, if widely announced, will create many transactions and will have a high visibility within the company. This will be particularly the case if many employees are invited to nominate/select employees for awards. HR will only be able to handle this process without need for additional headcount, if there is an easy-to-handle IT-solution in place which covers most of the transactions.

Part V
Compensation and Benefits

Introduction

William Eggers

Compensation is the loudest form of communication within your company. The business strategy needs to be supported and compensation and benefits are a strong way of doing so. Any misalignment will drive the company in the wrong direction.

Every compensation component has a different purpose. Make sure your employees understand the differences so that they are able to behave accordingly.

Compensation & Benefits are the single highest expenditure of a company (depending on the respective industry). Make sure your employees understand the value of the entire package, not just the cash components.

Benchmarking is a good way of understanding current market practice. However, it does not necessarily mean that you have to be like the market. Your decisions should be rather based on company needs and your specific business environment than just market practice.

Certain employee groups in your company can and probably should be managed and monitored on a global basis, e.g. your top executives. Here, certain compensation elements can be designed consistently to address this very target group. However, other groups of employees (e.g. tariff structures) need to be managed locally. Also, many benefits are purely local and follow local market needs.

The decision about what needs to be global and what needs to be local will also impact your processes and HR organization.

The times in which C&B basically determined salary increases and bonus payouts are over. The role has changed significantly to consult top management and be

W. Eggers (✉)
Frankfurt am Main, Germany
e-mail: DosDontsHR@yahoo.com

© Springer-Verlag Berlin Heidelberg 2015
M. Zeuch (ed.), *Dos and Don'ts in Human Resources Management*,
DOI 10.1007/978-3-662-43553-3_34

a major interface with Finance, Legal, Tax, etc. It has changed into a strategic role that has a strong impact on your cost base on the one hand and on attraction of top talent on the other. Make sure you have a C&B department in place that is able to play this important role within your company.

Job Evaluation

Konrad Reiher

Job Evaluation—What It Is and What It Is not!

For the top management "Job Evaluation=Work Measurement" is a process and tool to clarify executive roles and to show what kind of roles add what kind of value to the organization, based on the defined operating model and organizational design principles. It is a management tool and process, which generate clarity regarding roles, accountabilities and added value of executive and managerial jobs— a common view on the organizational set up and roles.

For HR professionals "Job Evaluation=Work Measurement" is a process and tool to understand and get deeper insights into organizations and job requirements which allows them to become a real HR business partner. The objective is to add real value to the further development of the organization based on the deep understanding of the business and organizational needs and to establish the backbone/ framework for a lot of HR processes like organizational design, talent management, placement decisions, HR controlling and reporting. It is the "iTunes" for HR professionals for their daily work.

"Job Evaluations=Work Measurement" is not a tool to benchmark compensation packages. Results can be used for this as well, but evaluating jobs only for this simple HR application is a very expensive and silly exercise.

K. Reiher (✉)
Bad Camberg, Germany
e-mail: DosDontsHR@yahoo.com

© Springer-Verlag Berlin Heidelberg 2015
M. Zeuch (ed.), *Dos and Don'ts in Human Resources Management*,
DOI 10.1007/978-3-662-43553-3_35

Management Involvement

"Job Evaluation = Work Measurement" is not a tool used by compensation experts "behind the curtain" and then confront the line management with the results. Top management should be involved into the whole process especially after restructuring of the organization or when the results will have significant impact to HR costs and individuals. Many well developed companies allocate the accountability for job evaluation to their Corporate Organizational Department, which is often part of Corporate Development & Strategies (as direct report to CEO).

Criteria to Be Used

For executive jobs the criteria should be focusing on business and functional governance, operating model and decision making processes as well as on accountabilities, impact of the job to the business and managerial requirements—the organizational set up and the expected added value from the executive job.

For single contributor the criteria should consider technical knowhow and skills, experience needed to perform the job as well as situations, which should be handled by the job.

The job evaluation system, which companies will use, should be able to cover the top job and the smallest job in the organization and should have a broad and global client base. Companies, using an internal tailor made tool, are struggling too often with the simplest and easiest application—compensation benchmarks. These companies often perform the job evaluation process twice—an expensive and silly exercise.

Benchmarking

Thomas Gruhle

Do Spend Some Time on Defining Your Peer Group

Companies tend to define the peer group by duplicating themselves (e.g. same region, same size, focusing on business competition). However, the comparator market for your talents might be different from the business competition. The question is to whom you lose your talents and where you hired them. Furthermore, location, industry, function and job size might have an impact on your reference market and vary by country.

Differentiate by Location

Salary and benefits practices and levels clearly vary by country (e.g. between emerging markets and established markets). Salary levels clearly vary by location (e.g. rural locations and urban locations).

T. Gruhle (✉)
Frankfurt am Main, Germany
e-mail: DosDontsHR@yahoo.com

© Springer-Verlag Berlin Heidelberg 2015
M. Zeuch (ed.), *Dos and Don'ts in Human Resources Management*,
DOI 10.1007/978-3-662-43553-3_36

Differentiate by Industry

Salary levels also vary significantly by industry. While global comparisons on a purely industry level are difficult, a better way to compare is by combining location and industry, for example "US American automotive industry" or "German chemical industry." For these clusters, benchmarking is important because talent is highly mobile within such clusters.

Differentiate by Function and Job Size

Some skills are very rare in the market and there will always be functions where pay needs to stay competitive. However, for some roles there are also opportunities to save money when recruiting. Make sure you have a common understanding of job requirements and content across the company. Most discussions ("We are not able to hire the talents we need for this money") happen because of a different understanding of job requirements. Involve line managers in the job sizing process as they have the best knowledge of the jobs.

Do Not Stop at Cash Compensation

Use a total remuneration approach rather than base salary comparisons. Even though your compensation & benefits package does not include a generous bonus, an attractive pension scheme or a company car—you should know whether your competitor's package these.

Do Benchmarking Regularly and Consistently

Compensation benchmarking should be done on a regular yearly basis. In fast emerging markets, a mid-year review can be advisable to keep pace with the market dynamics.

Benefits benchmarking does not need such a high frequency as compensation benchmarking, because benefits usually develop more gradually. As already mentioned in the chapter "Benefits", limiting the definition of benefits to those with clear monetary value allows for better comparison with other companies regarding the value of the total benefits package. This comparison can be used for employer marketing (if the package is generous) and for analyzing the company's cost position.

Don't Exchange Salary Data Directly with Competitors

This can be a violation of anti-trust laws. Prior to exchanging any tangible data with competition, you should make sure that this is in line with applicable laws.

Don't Use Cheap Data

Information about salary levels is available for free on the Internet. It could be tempting to use this information in order to save money on professional consultation. However, a diligent, professionally differentiated approach is necessary to find the right comparison.

- Make sure you use a source where data is delivered by HR professionals of the participating company only and not from employees.
- Professional providers will support you in job matching/job mapping meetings. If they don't know your organisation, how should they make sure your submission is correct?
- Choose a survey provider who collects individual data instead of average by job to ensure representation of the full dispersion of pay for the population.

Saving money in this area is like saving money on an oil change for a luxury car: it will cost you much more than you save today:

- If you don't pay enough for a certain job family and level, you will experience attrition of key talent.
- If you over-pay, your cost will be too high in comparison with your competitors.

Both mean high and unnecessary cost. A seemingly cheap solution can turn into a clear loss.

Do Challenge Your Survey Provider(s)

You need to become an informed survey customer to be able to interpret the market data from different providers.

- Your survey provider should be transparent about survey participants, the structure of the database, the used methodology as well as how data is collected, checked and processed. Question providers not asking you to submit data or offering a non-participating fee. Ask yourself: If they do the same with other customers as well, what do they upload to their databases?

- Do not focus too much on two or three peer companies on the participant list. Having one or two well-known companies on the participant list might help you with internal acceptance but in a valid data sample, the impact on market levels will be limited. Much more important is a representative number of companies within the chosen peer group parameters.
- Ask for support in interpretation of the data to find the right conclusions. Ask for local support to make sure you are aware of market specifics.

Do Benchmarking Internally as Well

Look at your internal consistency before benchmarking externally. Employees will be frustrated when they do not feel as appreciated as the co-worker doing the same job.

Don't Be Afraid if Pay Is Below the Market

When turnover rates are okay and you can still attract and retain the talents you need, this does not mean you have to increase salaries.

Base Salary

Andreas Hofmann

Check Your Base Salary Positioning Regularly

To avoid over or under payment, you need to regularly check your pay positioning in the relevant market (see benchmarking). Your local salaries need to reflect the relevant market in the respective country or industry.

Define Your Peer Group Carefully

Select your peer group carefully for your industry or your business divisions—in different markets you may compete with different companies (e.g. local players), this should be reflected in your system as well.

But do not be too narrow, otherwise, your available data sample might be too small or not stable enough.

Differentiate by Location and/or Industry

Salary levels vary by country and within countries by location, (e.g. rural locations tend to have lower salary levels than urban locations). Your base salary system must be flexible enough to allow for such local differentiation.

A. Hofmann (✉)
Frankfurt am Main, Germany
e-mail: DosDontsHR@yahoo.com

© Springer-Verlag Berlin Heidelberg 2015
M. Zeuch (ed.), *Dos and Don'ts in Human Resources Management*,
DOI 10.1007/978-3-662-43553-3_37

Check Local Rules and Regulations

In some countries, relevant rules for salary review exist that you need to reflect upon, such as minimum wage as well as mandatory annual increase linked to inflation rates. Check which rules apply locally.

Link Salary Movements to Performance and Market-Pay Ratios

Ensure a clear link to performance for the pay review: on company (budget) level as well as for the individual level. Your budget is usually based on company performance and expected market movement in addition to general economic information (e.g. inflation rate and development of Gross Domestic Product).

Differentiate individual salary increases based on performance and position of individuals vs. local market, however However, avoid too many intervals (simple matrix). The relative performance differentiation shouldn't be different between locations: e.g. same matrix with different absolute values based on local market, but same steps based on performance and relative position for all countries.

Top performers, who are already well positioned or paid above market are most difficult to handle. Think about one-off payments in order to motivate this population, but also keep your salary management system consistent for the future.

Define What You Want to Communicate Carefully

If you communicate full salary ranges, be aware that every employee would like to be at the maximum of the range. It's worth thinking about orientation values instead of minimum, midpoint and maximum for each range. Every pay system, which is aligned to your company's strategy as well as your employees' needs, is worth story telling. Consider how you can maximize your employees' appreciation of your specific pay system.

Bonus Plans

Thomas Haussmann

First Decide What You Want

Before going into the technical details of defining a bonus plan, first it is important to decide what kind of performance and behavior the company really wants. Here are some questions to ask:

- What do we want to reward for in the first place: company performance or individual performance—or good teamwork?
- Do we want more individual performers or more team players?
- What is key to our success: individual top performers or an increase of average performance?
- Do we want people who just achieve their targets or shall the *way* they achieve the targets play a role (e.g. leadership behavior, ethical behavior)?
- Do we want salespeople to drive revenue or profit?
- Do we want to drive sales of certain products more than other products, or is one dollar in sales as good as any other dollar in sales?

As can be seen from these questions, variable compensation is closely connected to the way the company is being led and steered. In other words: variable compensation has to follow company strategy!

T. Haussmann (✉)
Frankfurt am Main, Germany
e-mail: DosDontsHR@yahoo.com

© Springer-Verlag Berlin Heidelberg 2015
M. Zeuch (ed.), *Dos and Don'ts in Human Resources Management*,
DOI 10.1007/978-3-662-43553-3_38

Target vs. Actuals or Actuals vs. Actuals?

One of the fundamental questions of bonus plans is how to define success. Success can be exceeding a target ("target vs. actuals"). Success can also mean doing better this year than last year ("actuals vs. actuals"). In some cases, it means doing better than the competition ("actuals vs. peers").

In theory, the approach "target vs. actuals" is more fair, as it can, e.g., take into account the miserable economic situation in one country and the splendid growth situation in another. This requires an unbiased setting of the target. If this is not possible, "actuals vs. actuals" is more appropriate than assessing against a biased target.

Consider Overall Company Performance

If individual performance is the key issue to be fostered by the bonus plan, company performance should not play an overwhelming role in that plan. You cannot achieve both: motivate people to do as much as they can by promising them money for good performance and do not pay them any bonus if the company had a bad year.

If you want to make company performance a key element of the bonus plan, the impact of individual performance on the bonus is automatically—and significantly—reduced.

The simplest form of variable compensation for company performance is a flat bonus amount, identical for all employees. This is easy but may lead to high payouts for low-level jobs and insignificant amounts for top jobs. A graded approach is therefore more appropriate in many cases.

More elaborate forms of variable compensation include company performance placed in a formula with other factors such as team performance and individual performance.

Consider Team Performance

Taking into account team results—as opposed to purely rewarding individual performance or an anonymous company performance—can drive team cooperation. In today's world of work, it is hard to determine what really constitutes a team. Even though organizational structures formally define teams by departments, real-life cooperation can be completely different (e.g. the head of payroll, who is part of the HR team, might have more contact with the accounting team and the IT team than with HR's training and development team).

Consider Individual Performance

To measure individual performance, one option is to define measurable targets and calculate their achievement at year end ("management by objectives") or to rate the individual's achievements/behaviors. Some companies also include team feedback, customer feedback, etc. in the rating. Measurable targets can be defined for employees who have a measurable outcome of their work:

- sales persons who can be measured on sales volume or sales revenue, etc.
- blue collar workers who can be measured on output, quality, etc.
- call center agents who can be measured on number of solved issues, call volume, customer feedback, etc.
- internal recruiters who can be measured by the number of successful hires.

For those employees whose output cannot be quantified, qualitative targets must be defined. To create a certain objectivity, descriptions of what various levels of target achievement mean are helpful to prevent surprises at year end and to make clear to the individual what exactly is expected from him.

Make Achievements Transparent

As far as possible, company results which are part of the calculation of variable compensation should be transparent for employees throughout the year. This focuses attention on the overall development of the company and enhances identification with the company as a whole.

Regarding individual progress toward the goal, a mid-year review should create transparency. The year-end rating should not come as a complete surprise, especially if the rating is negative.

Don't Make It a Science

The deeper one thinks about variable compensation, the more complicated the systems become.

There is a level of complexity at which employees start to shut down and develop a "whatever" attitude towards the compensation scheme. Even if further differentiation makes sense, it should be tested whether the overall formulas can still be understood by non-experts.

There is one more reason to keep it simple: If you include many performance dimensions (company, division, team, individual)—or even all of them—in a variable pay plan, the impact of each dimension gets diluted. There is a danger to make the whole plan ineffective by overloading it with too many dimensions and objectives. Less is more: Concentrate on one dimension that is key for you, and on a few important objectives, and neglect the rest!

A good rule is the "elevator rule" (which applies for all HR policies): what you cannot explain in a normal elevator ride from ground floor to a mid-level floor, will not work.

Long-term Incentive Plans

Eric Engesaeth

Align with the Corporate Strategy

Strategy is typically defined as the determination of long-term goals and objectives, and the adoption of courses of action and the allocation of resources necessary for carrying out these goals. A perfect way to show confidence in the strategy is to link the long-term incentive ("LTI") plan to the goals and objectives in the strategic plan, i.e. "put your money where your mouth is."

Be Clear About the Role of Performance

The effectiveness of the design of the LTI plan can be greatly enhanced by being clear about the role of performance:

- Pay drives performance: if the primary goal is to influence people's behavior, it is vital that the LTI plan is structured in such a way that employees can influence the chosen performance metrics ("line of sight"). This typically involves executing an analysis of the most important underlying drivers of the strategic objectives and cascading these derived performance goals to the appropriate levels in the organization.

E. Engesaeth (✉)
Amsterdam, Netherlands
e-mail: DosDontsHR@yahoo.com

© Springer-Verlag Berlin Heidelberg 2015
M. Zeuch (ed.), *Dos and Don'ts in Human Resources Management*,
DOI 10.1007/978-3-662-43553-3_39

• Performance drives pay: if the primary goal is to legitimize pay based on achieved performance ("goal alignment"), the plan can be directly linked to the overall strategic objectives or for example a measure such as (relative) Total Shareholder Return. Most individuals will not be able to (directly) influence the outcome on these measures. It may therefore not create an effective *incentive*, but the plan could support other objectives, such as corporate glue, wealth creation, retention, etc.

Consider Different Payment Vehicles

LTI plans are often share-based payments. The basic payment vehicles are stock options vs. shares. An additional feature could be that the plan is settled in cash, i.e. stock appreciation rights (SARs) vs. phantom shares. Cash-settled share based payments sometimes have a cap (e.g. to prevent perceived excessive outcomes). The payment vehicle needs to fit the business profile and life-cycle of the company. Stock options may be effective in case of start-up/ high growth company but less effective otherwise.

Mind the Cost vs. Value Gap

When establishing the LTI policy, it goes without saying that it is important to carefully consider the funding, accounting costs, the impact on cash flow, overhang and dilution (limits) and corporate tax deductibility. However, this is only one side of the coin. The other side is the value to the recipient. Individual taxation is an important factor in various countries that sometimes even dominates the way plans are designed. However, here we are more generally talking about the "perceived value." The gap between the cost to the company and the perceived value to the recipient can be significant. The driver of the gap is the uncertainty about the reward. This "compensation risk" is, for example, higher if the performance volatility of the company is higher, but is also heavily influenced by the plan design and the degree of influence an individual employee has on the reward. A perceived value or "certainty equivalence" analysis is therefore recommended to fine-tune the design and bridge the gap.

Don't Overcomplicate

The road to a simple and understandable LTI plan is not an easy one. Simplifying LTI plans may involve considering simpler structures, fewer metrics, fewer legacy plans, etc. Especially for Main Board LTI plans, mandatory features are typical, for example due to governance or regulation. However, there is no need to cascade these sometimes complex reward features to the entire eligible population.

Restrict Eligibility

Making LTI available to too many people may lead to awards that are considered too small in light of the intended effect. It may further create a disproportional administrative burden.

Invest in Effective Communication

More transparency, disclosure and better communication greatly enhance the effectiveness of LTI plans. For internal communication purposes, it is recommended to *brand* the LTI plan and operate a platform where employees can have easy access to the current (and potential future) status of their awards and the associated wealth. The external communication strategy aims to show the added value to shareholders and other stakeholders and to prevent reputational damage, e.g. as a result of top executive realized LTI compensation.

Benefits

Lisa Emerson and Yvonne Prang

Do Have a Global Competitive Positioning Target for the Overall Benefit Package

Within your global Rewards strategy or framework, you need to have a competitive target position for the overall Benefit package that reflects how you want your programs to compare against your competitor group. Leave enough freedom within the framework to allow for local relevance.

Do Know What Everyone Else is Offering—and then Differentiate

Your local programs need to reflect the relevant market in the respective country or industry. So have a good understanding what the most common benefits in the local market are that all employers offer. And then differentiate your benefits offerings by choosing the one or two element(s) that make you unique. You might even consider having a globally common program that makes you stand out from the rest and that you deliver wherever legally possible.

L. Emerson (✉)
Glen Ellyn, IL, USA
e-mail: DosDontsHR@yahoo.com

Y. Prang
Munich, Germany
e-mail: DosDontsHR@yahoo.com

© Springer-Verlag Berlin Heidelberg 2015
M. Zeuch (ed.), *Dos and Don'ts in Human Resources Management*,
DOI 10.1007/978-3-662-43553-3_40

Do Check Local Rules and Regulations

Most countries offer tax advantages and/or deduction of expenses for some benefits. If you want to take advantage of those advantages, you need to be very mindful of the rules and regulations that you may need to build into a program. Check which rules apply locally and make sure you follow them very closely.

Do Think Win–Win

Identify the different target groups you have in your organization. Have an idea of the perceived value that those different target groups place on the benefit(s) you offer to them. Also, do a thorough analysis of the cost the particular program bears for you as an employer. The best programs are those that the employees in the target group place a high value on, but that don't cost the company a lot of money. Also, look for opportunities to provide employees access to a benefit at lower cost than the employee can "buy" it on the external market—even get a tax advantage—and you have a win–win situation.

Do Focus—Less Is More

Don't try to cater to everyone by doing a little bit of everything. Focus on the elements with the highest perceived value by the respective employee target group which you can deliver at low or reasonable cost. Do less, but then do that right!

Don't Take a One- Size- Fits- All Approach

Don't assume what works very well in one country will also work as well in another country. People's preferences and applicable laws do differ. Respecting local market practices and employee preferences is already really important, but even more vital the tax and legal compliance of your programs in each country.

Don't Underestimate the Need for Communication and Education

Most tax efficient benefit programs are—at least in the eye of the employee—highly complicated. All your employees need to understand those programs to appreciate what you are doing for them. Simply handing over all the small print to them to read will not lead to the desired results, especially if—for example in a matching plan—employees have to put up their own money in order to receive an employer contribution. You need to explain in an easy to understand language what the benefit is all about, and what exactly is in for them if they participate. Even if you are dealing with a very complicated topic, find a way to communicate in simple and easy to understand language. When communicating, always put yourself in the place of the employee and not in the place of the HR professional. Avoid making anything complicated and ensure that participation as easy as possible for employees.

Expatriate Management/International Assignment Policy

Jürgen Czajor

Start with Expectation Management

Sending Executives or Specialists on an international assignment should create a win–win situation. The company needs the assignee to implement its international business strategy; the employee gets an attractive development opportunity in his/her professional career, very often for the whole family. Before starting an assignment, therefore it is important that employees not only understand the expectation of the management but also have answers for themselves. "What's in for me?" should include both the career perspective and the benefit package.

Global Policy for Local Execution

More than in any other area, the International Assignee Policy needs a clear agenda, transparent guidelines and as few changes as possible. The reason is that it has to be understood and executed by all HR departments of the company all over the world. Even though there might be a central department coordinating international policy execution, there will always be a part left for local HR. For local HR, however, international assignee topics are not day-to-day routine, so the more complicated the policy is and the more frequent changes apply to it, the higher the risk that locally it is interpreted differently and that unequal treatments happen.

J. Czajor (✉)
Beijing, China
e-mail: DosDontsHR@yahoo.com

© Springer-Verlag Berlin Heidelberg 2015
M. Zeuch (ed.), *Dos and Don'ts in Human Resources Management*,
DOI 10.1007/978-3-662-43553-3_41

Better Big and Flat

The many big and small problems that come up when working abroad motivate companies to provide a set of monetary and nonmonetary benefits:

- A home flight to keep in touch with family, friends and the old department.
- A move allowance to ship the household goods to the new location.
- An electric allowance to buy electronics in a country with different voltage.
- A kitchen equipment allowance, and so on.

Detailed assignment policies with a multitude of benefits and allowances and complicated reimbursement processes with physical receipts are a massive administrative burden for Home- and Host-HR. Such benefits are like going to a supermarket only with coupons: one cannot buy the things one needs but only the things that can be purchased with the coupons.

This is why allowances should focus on typical situations like relocation and not describe in detail items that can be reimbursed. Allowances should be packed and operated as one time or monthly cash payments depending on easy to administer criteria, such as measurable criteria and steps happened, number of children or hierarchy.

Don't Sell the Story that All Differences in Cost and Living Will Be Compensated

Some companies tend to develop policies that should compensate any difference in cost and living compared with the assignees' home country. This culture very often leads to a comprehensive cover mindset and results in unpleasant discussions about small money. A state of the art policy should firstly ensure that the expatriate is provided a net-base package ensuring he/she has the same buying power as at home. Secondly a set of generous benefits should support housing, schooling, healthcare, relocation and mobility and special local hardship but not tend to cover each small item which the expatriate might miss—e.g. special kitchen equipment or maintenance of highly specific appliances.

Don't Underestimate the Emotional Part

People on international assignment usually face additional stress:

- Family-related issues such as kindergarten and schooling.
- The expectation of the accompanying spouse.
- Language problems and cultural adjustment.
- Simple day-to-day life issues like set-up private phone and internet connection, repairs in the household.

Even usually resilient, senior employees can become quite emotional in such situations which put them far off their comfort zone. This is why, for HR, it is of highly important not to add to this stress level with policy-related uncertainties, delayed payments and intransparent reimbursement processes. Think about a buddy-program where an experiences assignee acts as a mentor for the newcomer in the on-boarding weeks.

Don't Underestimate International Taxation

For international assignees, not only the local tax liability but also the tax liabilities from the home country or other former countries of assignment can apply. Examples are not only long lasting stock option plans or bonus payments from previous years. Company car and driver, business club memberships, dinner invitations with life partners might not be taxable in the host country, while in the home country they are taxable. Because they are tax-free in the host country, there is most often no reporting process installed to track this. An expat, however, might still be tax liable towards his home country (e.g. in the year of transition) and hence his home tax declaration should include the mentioned items. This means HR and F/C in the host country have to develop a process wherein such items are completely reported and available for taxation in the assignees host- and home country.

Part VI
Administration and Payroll

Introduction

Matthias Zeuch

This area encompasses all operative processes which are necessary to employ people. It starts with entering new employees into the company's systems, capturing all changes regarding the employment conditions for the employee (e.g. salary, work time, location, benefits eligibilities) and ensuring that all these are being accurately followed up with (e.g. payment of salary, granting of benefits, data reporting and taxation).

This is where HR historically comes from and is still the foundation of HR work. If HR fails to deliver high quality in these basics, it will lose credibility as guardian for all other HR practice areas!

Depending on the organizational structure of the HR department, HR IT systems and HR process management can also fall under this area.

M. Zeuch (✉)
Beijing, China
e-mail: DosDontsHR@yahoo.com

© Springer-Verlag Berlin Heidelberg 2015
M. Zeuch (ed.), *Dos and Don'ts in Human Resources Management*,
DOI 10.1007/978-3-662-43553-3_42

HR IT Systems

Matthias Zeuch

Use Self-Services and Self-Updates

Open system access for employees to obtain information and update (for example, their mailing address) on their own. This can create major capacity savings in HR administration.

Focus on User-Friendliness

While HR people use HR systems frequently, other employees and managers use the systems only a few times per year. If the system lacks user-friendliness and is not self-explanatory, HR administration will have to help users operate the system because they tend to struggle with the system every time they use it. This means that there will be no major saving in administrative workload for HR.

Avoid Data Redundancy

Do base all HR IT applications in one set of core employee data. Do not allow multiple data pools with the same type of information.

M. Zeuch (✉)
Beijing, China
e-mail: DosDontsHR@yahoo.com

© Springer-Verlag Berlin Heidelberg 2015
M. Zeuch (ed.), *Dos and Don'ts in Human Resources Management,*
DOI 10.1007/978-3-662-43553-3_43

Cheap Can Be Expensive

Even though it might be tempting to let a talented intern quickly program an HR IT solution you always wanted to have, it is highly advisable not to allow the creation of "self-made" HR IT solutions without professional standards such as documentation, compatibility to other systems, data safety and data security standards. Once the person who created the "self-made" solution leaves the company, maintenance of the system will be impossible and all work entered in the system might be in vain. Lack of standards of data protection can lead to legal problems in certain countries.

HR Process Management

Matthias Zeuch

Map HR Process

HR process mapping sets a professional standard in HR management, which

- serves new colleagues in HR as a reference when learning their jobs.
- allows documentation of all HR compliance requirements and ISO requirements.
- clarifies roles and responsibilities/avoids repeated territorial discussions.
- shows non-HR people interfacing with HR what they can expect (and what not to expect) and how their interaction with HR should be.
- makes HR audit-proof—certainly under the pre-condition that all HR staff follow the processes as described.

Mind the Workload

It takes a significant effort for HR to build and maintain an HR process map. This is why it has to be defined as project with dedicated resources, and it should not come just on top of existing tasks.

M. Zeuch (✉)
Beijing, China
e-mail: DosDontsHR@yahoo.com

© Springer-Verlag Berlin Heidelberg 2015
M. Zeuch (ed.), *Dos and Don'ts in Human Resources Management,*
DOI 10.1007/978-3-662-43553-3_44

Combine with Education in HR

To enhance attractiveness and usage of process maps, a user-friendly, educational interface to the process maps can be advisable. Such an interface translates the major contents into easy-to-understand language and uses a "Dos/Don'ts" structure to highlight the major consequences for the user.

Carefully Select IT Systems

The more complex your HR processes are, the higher the necessity of a professional IT system is to handle process documentation.

Take Time to Create Top-Level Processes

Changing the top-level structure after determining the detailed topics/processes is painful and time intensive. It is advisable to go through all details before, cluster them, and then define the right top-down structure.

Think About a User-Friendly Interface

As already mentioned under „HR IT Systems", such an interface might create higher acceptance and usage of the process map.

Don't Underestimate Acceptance Problems

Most HR people do not have a technical background and are not comfortable with highly detailed descriptions of how they should do their work. With early introduction of the HR process map (shortly after the on-boarding process), acceptance can be increased.

Heike Hartrath

Be Aware of the "Outsourcing Threat"

If you decide to outsource, make sure that you minimize internal resistance by implementing a change management process which involves the people (HR employees and the business) affected by this decision. Try to proactively deal with insecurities and address potential benefits.

Ensure a Realistic Balance of Quality Expectations and Cost Reductions

Outsourcers may offer easy-to-realize cost reductions by relying on better scale effects and significantly lower labor costs. Make sure they also come with a broad experience/best practices, proven IT systems, and professional processes. This will ensure a service delivery on or even above previous internal service levels.

H. Hartrath (✉)
Berlin, Germany
e-mail: DosDontsHR@yahoo.com

© Springer-Verlag Berlin Heidelberg 2015
M. Zeuch (ed.), *Dos and Don'ts in Human Resources Management,*
DOI 10.1007/978-3-662-43553-3_45

143

Explore Opportunities for Shared Services Before Outsourcing

Together with other internal HR departments, seize all opportunities of internal optimization without territorial envy to show business management that you are able to deliver HR services at benchmark cost level.

Consider Reasonable Outsourcing

Outsourcers may be able to deliver routine services such as payroll and related HR administration processes at lower cost than your internal HR department. This potentially gives your HR department the chance to completely focus on strategically important HR topics.

Require Documentation and Back-up Capacity from Outsources

Some outsourcers have a high turnover because they keep salaries low. This is why a good level of automation, up-to-date documentation and back-up capacities are important to avoid disruption in base processes.

Don't Underestimate the Need for Retained Capacity

When calculating a business case for outsourcing, do not forget that there might still be a need for retained capacities. The smaller the units in which you need these, the higher the potential that the business case becomes negative.

Example:

If you have a large payroll department with 20 employees and the need for one retained person for company-specific, complicated issues, the overall business case will most likely be positive and relatively easy to accomplish.

On the other hand, if you have a payroll department with only two people, and one of them needs to be retained, the business case for outsourcing will probably not be positive.

Payroll

Matthias Zeuch

Monitor Performance

Performance of payroll can be measured with error quota, customer satisfaction rate and delayed payments. Due to the connection to employee satisfaction, these measurements are important to track and report.

Avoid Cryptic Pay Slips

Some pay slips look like products of the early ages of computer technology. Cryptic numeric codes and abbreviations, pages of confusing re-calculations and a format which does not provide any logical structure to people outside the payroll department. Work with non-payroll people to create understandable pay slips.

Use Pay Slips for Employee Communication

The pay slip is a document most employees read on a monthly basis. Hence, it provides the company with an easy channel to communicate to employees. Reserve space in the design of the pay slip and communicate not only payroll-related topics

M. Zeuch (✉)
Beijing, China
e-mail: DosDontsHR@yahoo.com

© Springer-Verlag Berlin Heidelberg 2015
M. Zeuch (ed.), *Dos and Don'ts in Human Resources Management,*
DOI 10.1007/978-3-662-43553-3_46

but also other topics to employees via this cost-free channel. If the technical set-up allows, also use colors to make the pay slip more attractive.

Train Payroll Staff in Customer Service

Payroll staff is in frequent interaction with employees, they are major representatives of the company towards the employees. This is why for payroll staff customer-oriented behavior should be trained and incentives/performance evaluations should be defined accordingly.

Part VII
HR Governance and Compliance

Introduction

Julia Borggraefe

When doing business, companies must abide by applicable laws and rules. Furthermore, companies are more and more expected to be "fair" and "transparent" from the perspective of civil society.

Therefore, on the one hand companies develop monitoring systems to make sure they act compliant, on the other hand they define their own catalogues of rules and guidelines to ensure internal consistency, fairness and transparency and external reliability, professionalism and quality. If a company has branches in different countries and/or different divisions, a major question is how far these internal rules and guidelines are binding for all countries/divisions or if those units are allowed to create their own. One of the big challenges therefore is to find a level that is globally applicable.

While HR governance describes the active part of steering major sensitive areas of HR (for example, compensation and benefits for executives, expatriates and sometimes middle-management, performance management, major rules of conduct, labor relations), HR compliance means processes to ensure that both the external and the internal rules are being followed (= "complied with").

J. Borggraefe (✉)
Berlin, Germany
e-mail: DosDontsHR@yahoo.com

© Springer-Verlag Berlin Heidelberg 2015
M. Zeuch (ed.), *Dos and Don'ts in Human Resources Management*,
DOI 10.1007/978-3-662-43553-3_47

Business Ethics

Josef Wieland

Make Ethics and Values Tangible

When communicating about business ethics and company values, be as concrete as possible. General statements and philosophical terms will not help real-life implementation of ethics and values in a company. Concrete examples with a clear positioning of the company ("No, we will never accept discrimination between groups of people" and "Yes, we have policies on equal work—equal pay" and "Yes we encourage whistle-blowing and also protect the whistleblowers") make it much more tangible.

Demonstrate Ethical Behavior Top–down

The "tone from the top" as well as corresponding behavior of top management is essential for a sustainable application of values and ethical behavior in the whole organization. People have to feel that it is not "just said" but "really meant."

J. Wieland (✉)
Friedrichshafen, Germany
e-mail: DosDontsHR@yahoo.com

© Springer-Verlag Berlin Heidelberg 2015
M. Zeuch (ed.), *Dos and Don'ts in Human Resources Management*,
DOI 10.1007/978-3-662-43553-3_48

Train the Decision Makers

Ethical behavior is understood differently by each person and hence an organization must sensitize and train its decision makers, to achieve coherence in its value systems. This translates into implementing Integrity management programs to sensitize and update the managers around the world on the latest standards on corporate responsibility and corporate governance.

Adapt the Incentive Structures to Your Values

The corporate values would never get implemented in everyday business life if the recruitment and incentive structures do not match it. The employees' motivation to adhere to the firm's values must be in resonance with the personal financial implications of their decision making.

Communicate Regularly and Openly to the Stakeholders

The stakeholders should know the efforts made by the company to meet the standards of corporate responsibility and governance. It should go beyond glossy brochures with smiling faces and talk about the goals set for corporate responsibility, the results achieved and an explanation for non-achievement. In addition to winning their trust, such communication helps in fostering cooperation and support from the key stakeholders, especially in times of crisis.

Do Not Reduce It Just to "Compliance"

Do not suggest in your communication that formal compliance is the only important aspect of ethical behavior. As long as ethical conduct means following laws, rules and regulations, it is merely "compliant behavior." Integrity Management should be aimed at, at all levels of management to inculcate a sense of integrity from top management to the lowest level of decision making. The real-life proof of ethical intentions and ethical behavior, however, is if:

- there are no laws, rules or regulations governing the decision and/or,
- ethical aspects are in conflict with applicable laws, rules or regulations and/or,
- the decision is in conflict with other targets, e.g. financial targets.

Don't Forget Cultural Differences When Communicating

While the core values of your company should be universal, do not copy and paste respective communication tools from your home/HQ country to the rest of the world. Some examples are just not understood in other cultures.

Don't Overpromise

The more one communicates as "the most responsible firm caring for the environment and the society" ,the more the stakeholders' and the general public's expectation would be. This could seriously damage credibility for the slightest intransigence.

Policies and Guidelines

Nicola Mackin

Cover All Areas

Usually HR areas which are regulated by policies and labor guidelines are:

- Regular work time regulations.
- Individual work time regulations (temporary part-time after maternity leave or in case of severe family/health issues etc.).
- Vacation regulations
- Regulations regarding handling of contract workers (i.e. non-internal employees)
- Regulations & conditions regarding paid leave (sick leave, maternity leave, marriage leave etc.)
- Regulations & conditions regarding unpaid leave (extended maternity leave, sabbatical etc.)
- Company compensation schemes (fix & variable)
- Company Benefits scheme (company car, child care, company shares etc.)
- Safety and security regulations
- Travel regulations (transportation, accommodation, travel cost reimbursement, work & travel hours etc.)
- Company code of conduct (company & private rights, ethical behavior, corporate values, dress code etc.)

N. Mackin (✉)
Stuttgart, Germany
e-mail: DosDontsHR@yahoo.com

© Springer-Verlag Berlin Heidelberg 2015
M. Zeuch (ed.), *Dos and Don'ts in Human Resources Management,*
DOI 10.1007/978-3-662-43553-3_49

155

- Protection of company assets and corporate data (user rights management, user own devices, anti-trust regulations etc.)
- Corporate controls environment
- Handling of violations against corporate and/or local guidelines

Depending on your type of business and local specifics (culture, law), other areas might be added.

Mind Both Internal Rules and External Rules

All policies and labor guidelines, including disciplinary actions in case of violations, have to comply with the country's labor law as well as with all other applicable external rules and regulations (e.g. union agreements) and have to be regularly reviewed and updated as necessary. Particularly, the company cannot implement company policies with less regulation than legally required locally or even which are less favorable for the employees. Example: If minimum vacation days by law are 5 days per year, a company may decide to grant 10 days of minimum vacation, but not 4 days.

Changes in Policies and Labor Guidelines

HR will often be owner of policies and labor guidelines and will initiate additions/ changes if necessary. Legally it will be the local Board of Management to hold responsible for complying with company and local regulations/policies; HR will advise the BoM and ensure internal communication to executives and employees as necessary.

Furthermore, redundant or obsolete policies can be discontinued if appropriate.

As an example for a common company regulation to be implemented & communicated: with the growing importance of the internet and particularly social media in people's lives, companies have to determine in how far they allow employees to surf the Internet during work time for private purposes.

Make Transparent and Always Accessible at All Times

During their on-boarding period, all employees should be informed about the existing policies and labor guidelines and specific implications for them in their roles.

All policies & guidelines should be stored in an easily accessible repository (e.g. "Employee Handbook") for employees to find all applicable rules and regulations, preferably in the intranet of the company. Also, all executives and employees should be informed about relevant changes in policies and labor guidelines.

HR Compliance

Eckart Jensen

Ensure Legal and Process Compliance at All Times

All employment-related laws and regulations have to be transparent and up-to-date:

1. Directly employment-related external rules such as: Employment Law, Diversity and Discrimination laws, Privacy Data Protection Law, regulations to set up a Union, Tax regulations, Social Security or other mandatory insurances and Immigration regulations.
2. External rules and regulations with impact on HR practices (e.g. Anti Money Laundering or Anti Bribery laws).
3. Internal rules, regulations, policies or procedures.

Integrate HR Compliance into the Whole HR Value Chain

All relevant aspects of HR Compliance need to be part of the HR core processes (e.g. staffing, compensation, benefits, succession planning, performance management, payroll, HR Admin, and HR IT).

E. Jensen (✉)
Singapore, Singapore
e-mail: DosDontsHR@yahoo.com

© Springer-Verlag Berlin Heidelberg 2015
M. Zeuch (ed.), *Dos and Don'ts in Human Resources Management*,
DOI 10.1007/978-3-662-43553-3_50

Drive a Compliance Culture Within the Organization

The importance of a compliant business culture needs to be highlighted in company events; department meetings and role models should be honored (e.g. HR Compliance Award).

Do Targeted and Customized Communication

HR Compliance consists of legal and process compliance. Global, transnational, local and organizational rules and regulations have to be taken into consideration. The communication has to be target group specific and all media have to be used to bring the message in a short and memorable way across.

Do Regular Risk Assessment/HR Compliance Self-assessment

The organization needs to know the respective status of the HR Compliance Program and perform a fit-gap analysis. The HR risk assessment should be performed annually to determine if the risks are critical to the success of the organization. A plan with remedial actions needs to be developed and implemented.

Have a Transparent Set of Rules and Regulations in Case of Violations

It needs to be clear to every employee, agency worker and supplier how the organization treats violations. Compliance violations have to be notified and - if required - punished without exception.

Don't Use Non-compliance as Excuse

We often hear the following argument related to high-risk countries: "The compliance rules and regulations are blocking us from successful business." Data show that compliant organizations have a higher shareholder return, higher profits and lower operating costs (esp. in HR).

Don't Exclude Individuals or Employee Groups from the Scope

HR Compliance refers to all employees in the company and includes even agency workers, contractors and third party vendors with special compliance regulations. All employees should be treated in the same and constant way.

Don't Say: "HR Compliance Is Expensive"

The implementation of compliant business practices and behavior is a part of the leadership task. Only the setup of an HR Compliance function, the implementation of additional monitoring and tracking systems might require additional funding. The cost of being non-compliant (law suits and penalties) is much higher (e.g. penalties for breaches of the Privacy Data Protection).

Don't Do a "Little Bit" of HR Compliance

The implementation of HR Compliance requires a full comprehensive approach. An implementation of only selected parts will leave the employees in uncertainty and expose the organization to risks.

HR Audit and Investigations

Bernhard Balz

Handle and Communicate with Care

Both HR audits and investigations are activities with high sensitivity. At times, audits have the potential to turn into individual investigations. Those who are subject to audits or investigations might interpret the audit/investigation as a lack of trust in their motives and actions.

On the other hand, only with trust the company leadership would not fulfill its obligation to safeguard the company's interest. Investors want to be sure that their investment is in good hands. If, for example, decisions of a purchasing manager are influenced by bribes, the decisions will certainly not be in the best interest of the investor.

Sensitive communication to all those involved is of utmost importance, to do what is necessary and not destroy motivation of employees who did nothing wrong.

A piece of advice to all those who have to communicate this is the analogy of a suspected dangerous illness in the body: the best thing to do is a complete examination in order to make the most accurate diagnosis, and not to avoid certain tests just because they cause some pain.

B. Balz (✉)
Nuertingen, Germany
e-mail: DosDontsHR@yahoo.com

© Springer-Verlag Berlin Heidelberg 2015
M. Zeuch (ed.), *Dos and Don'ts in Human Resources Management*,
DOI 10.1007/978-3-662-43553-3_51

Give the Utmost Support

All concerned HR employees should give all needed/requested information and
their valuable input during the audit process and help to set up a treatment plan.
Otherwise it is not possible to gain a common understanding of the situation and
the root causes of process weaknesses and risks. It is also not possible to uncover
any unfavourable conditions, misalignments with operational goals and incompli-
ance with laws, regulations and policies. Only the experts of HR together with the
auditors are able to find the best solution and agreed actions to remediate those
risks and weaknesses.

Do Not Forget the Debrief

After audits and investigations, those who were screened deserve information
about the findings and agreements. This information should be given as soon as
it is releasable.

Part VIII
HR Strategy and Change

Introduction

Oliver Grohmann

HR Strategy

The HR strategy provides the direction and priorities for the people-related work of the company.

It should consist of both

a. Goal statements regarding the desired workforce (e.g. highly motivated and engaged people in the company, best people for the job, competitive workforce) or the employer image of the company (e.g. attractive place to work) and

b. Goal statements about the HR work within the company (e.g. highly efficient HR processes, high service orientation of HR).

The objective of these two areas is the same, to ensure the success of the organization! While the goals under (b) can and should be steered directly by HR, goals under (a) can only be achieved jointly between HR and the management team of an organization. This means that major HR goals are not just the job of the HR department but a team effort!

O. Grohmann (✉)
Singapore, Singapore
e-mail: DosDontsHR@yahoo.com

© Springer-Verlag Berlin Heidelberg 2015
M. Zeuch (ed.), *Dos and Don'ts in Human Resources Management*,
DOI 10.1007/978-3-662-43553-3_52

Change Management

Change management means coordinated and structured activities to support major changes in the company, with the objective to ensure successful execution and sustainable results. It is not 'the soft stuff', but has a huge impact on the success of an organization!

Activities vary significantly and are strongly dependent on the framework, the organization, etc. They should be specific and focused, and can include interviews for stakeholder analysis, and conducting management workshops, together with roll-out support and communication campaigns.

Change management is one of the newer types of HR activities, and one of the most underestimated. By far not all HR departments provide (and can provide) this type of service. With the increasing speed and impact of changes in all areas, it is essential for a sustainable success of an organization to be ahead of the game! Economic crises, unexpected growth, sudden changes in regulatory environments, ground-breaking new technologies become frequent game-changers. Exception becomes the norm. HR is usually in the "eye of the storm" and should understand that change management is an integral part of their role.

HR Strategy

Oliver Grohmann

Align HR Strategy with Overall Company Strategy and Market

The only objective of an HR strategy is to drive the success of the organization. It should be needless to say that it therefore has to be closely aligned with the business strategy.

Bring Your Own Topics to the Table

Of course, the people topics in the strategy must be derived from the business strategy! However, it is insufficent to purely describe the goals based on the business goals. You are the expert if it comes to People topics, and the management expects that you advise which topics should be considered and tackled, e.g. the fact of changing expectations and behaviors of the younger generation, and the related need for flexible workplace solutions must come from you!

O. Grohmann (✉)
Singapore, Singapore
e-mail: DosDontsHR@yahoo.com

© Springer-Verlag Berlin Heidelberg 2015
M. Zeuch (ed.), *Dos and Don'ts in Human Resources Management*,
DOI 10.1007/978-3-662-43553-3_53

Describe Goals for Both, the HR Function and the Organization

Get your house in order, describe what is needed to get an effective and efficient HR organization; this is your responsibility in a first step. However, the part with the higher impact on the overall organization is to describe the people goals in general. This can only be developed and executed in a close collaboration between HR and the management.

Don't Underestimate Buy-in and Communication

Of course, the content of an HR Strategy is important. However, I have seen a lot of HR Strategies which address the right topic, but without the full buy-in and support of the (TOP-) Management and the HR organization it will never fly! Spend sufficient time with the management and the HR organization at the early stage of developing a strategy. Involve as many as possible colleagues in a structured way, and ensure that it is their strategy and their language that are used.

I strongly recommend that you ask for a strong commitment of the (TOP-) Management and ask for some concrete strategic decisions regarding HR. This will allow the HR leader to set priorities for his/her team.

Questions like the following can bring the necessary clarity and turn a one-size-fits-all HR strategy into a real-life HR strategy for your company:

- If you could pick one people topic that ensures the success of the organization, what would that be?
- Do we want a 'family feeling' or internal competition?
- Do we want to be average or premium in compensation and benefits?
- Do we believe in an 'elite approach' in talent management or a broad approach?
- Do we believe in diversity of leadership teams?
- Do we believe in empowerment of local leaders?

Don't Make It Too General, but Focus on the Specific Situation

It goes without saying that the HR strategy cannot be changed yearly, but it should connect to the specific situation of the organization to ensure successful implementation. Please find the following two examples which could be applied in case of growth/declining markets.

Example 1: HR Strategy for a Growth Market "Support the Planned Growth of Our Business"

- HR Marketing: Become one of the top ten employers in our industry.
- Recruiting: Use best-in-class selection tools, as well as internships, to hire the best possible people for our company.
- Training: Ensure fast and effective on-boarding of new hires. Train new leaders to cope with the fast growth of their responsibility.
- Compensation: Ensure that in key job families our compensation level is significantly above market average.
- Engagement/Retention: Drive retention of all capable staff.
- HR Administration: Introduce new IT systems to be prepared for handling a significantly larger workforce.

Example 2: HR Strategy for a Declining Market "Keep the Lights on in Times of Crisis and Retain Top Performers"

- Training: Find methods to reduce training cost via today's IT capabilities.
- Train leaders to motivate in times of crisis.
- Compensation: Compensate for top performance.
- Engagement/Retention: Identify key people and develop a selective retention strategy for them.
- HR Administration: Identify and realize saving opportunities in HR operations.

Don't Forget to Measure

Ideally use a Balanced Score Card or similar tool to break down the strategic goals into measurable targets. Track the progress of the achievements and report them to the Top Management. This will draw attention to people topics and make it easier for the HR leader to get approval for necessary decisions and investments.

Matthias Zeuch

Furnish Your HR Team Members with Arguments and Reasons

HR team members are at times in a situation where they have to communicate new policies and regulations. Particularly if these policies are controversial, HR team members have to get prepared for discussions with their internal customers by sharing with them the reasons for implementation of the new rule.

To get a real-life impression between an uninformed HR team member and an informed HR team member, imagine the following two different statements of an HR team member towards a department head:

a. "I also do not understand this new rule from HQ. I think it is better you just follow the rule."
b. "I understand that this new rule will not make life easier for you. There were, however, several incidents in the company in which the following happened:... This is why HQ decided to implement this new rule."

M. Zeuch (✉)
Beijing, China
e-mail: DosDontsHR@yahoo.com

© Springer-Verlag Berlin Heidelberg 2015
M. Zeuch (ed.), *Dos and Don'ts in Human Resources Management*,
DOI 10.1007/978-3-662-43553-3_54

Do Plan and Execute a Waterfall Communication on Important Topics

Water-falling of information means that you start from the top level over middle management down to employee level.

If you ignore this waterfall by informing employees prior to middle management, you can almost bet that you will receive angry calls and emails from middle management about why they have not been informed prior to their employees. The reason for their dissatisfaction is that employees came to them wanting to discuss the new policy, and they, as the managers, had no idea what their employees were talking about.

Don't Forget to Talk About Your Achievements

One of the most typical mistakes HR departments make is to deliver a lot of value-added to the company but remain too humble to talk about it. HR has to find a good mix of "do good and talk about it", otherwise there is a tendency to measure HR only on things that go wrong.

A regular HR report in which achievements, key performance indicators and open issues are presented to top management can help create this balance. For the broader audience of all employees in the company, HR can use a newsletter, the intranet or HR participation in a town-hall meeting to report on successes and achievements.

Don't Underestimate the Impact of Your Statements

As an HR person, you are seen by most employees not only as a colleague but also as a representative of the HR department. A personal statement might resurface as, "HR thinks that …" in the organization.

Business Partnership

Matthias Zeuch

Mutual Respect

As in all partnerships, there are times of harmony and times of disagreement. As long as both sides value the position of the other, listen to each other and treat each other with respect, the final outcome will be better than a single decision by only one of the partners. In the end, it is about a joint decision in the best interest of the company.

Understand the Needs of Your Partner in Business

As a business partner, you have to understand the challenges and priorities your partners in business have. You will only be able to come up with the right HR solutions if you develop a deeper understanding of the processes and priorities of your partners in business. Based on this knowledge, you will be able to effectively develop, in cooperation with your business partner, selection criteria for candidates, development programs and drive specific leadership qualities within this area.

M. Zeuch (✉)
Beijing, China
e-mail: DosDontsHR@yahoo.com

© Springer-Verlag Berlin Heidelberg 2015
M. Zeuch (ed.), *Dos and Don'ts in Human Resources Management,*
DOI 10.1007/978-3-662-43553-3_55

Frequent Communication

Even though almost nobody wants to have more regular appointments in their calendar, try to do this with your partners in business. If you wait until you learn that there is an urgent need, you may already have lost time for proactively addressing it. In frequent conversations, you will be able to "hear the grass growing".

Don't Try to "Sell" to Your Partners in Business

Before developing HR products, listen to the needs of your partners in business. Do not try the opposite: invent something new in an ivory tower and then try to convince them about it.

Change Management

Matthias Zeuch

Holistic Approach

Change management should start with a holistic analysis of the as-is-situation and the desired outcome of the change process regarding:

- Major stakeholders and their interests
- Emotions about the change
- All relevant economic aspects
- Potential risks and their likelihood
- Operative consequences of the change.

Once having gained a complete picture, it is the goal of change management to support the successful transition from the as-is-situation to the desired state. If the necessary activities are mainly HR related (people selection, training, leadership development, employee communication), HR should take a leadership role in the change process.

M. Zeuch (✉)
Beijing, China
e-mail: DosDontsHR@yahoo.com

© Springer-Verlag Berlin Heidelberg 2015
M. Zeuch (ed.), *Dos and Don'ts in Human Resources Management,*
DOI 10.1007/978-3-662-43553-3_56

Ensure Change Management Capabilities

Whether you should develop change management capabilities internally or develop a relationship with trusted vendors for this, depends on frequency/intensity of change processes within your company, as well as the current level of skills in the HR team.

Either way, if HR wants to be more than "staff administration", it should be as close as possible to the major change processes in the company and be able to play a major role in change processes.

Don't Underestimate the Operational Aspects of Change

Sometimes, very operational issues can hinder the success of strategically well-designed change processes. Do not shy away from asking simple questions like:

- Will our IT system be able to handle this?
- Do we have enough space in our buildings for this?

Don't Underestimate Inter-Cultural Aspects

In any change process that includes people from different cultures, the necessary time and effort to ensure effective communication and mutual acceptance is usually much higher than originally estimated.

Mind the Waterfall Effect

Usually, change processes are discussed in small circle meetings of top management, prior to a broad communication. Often, such discussions take long exchanges of arguments. Once top management has found an agreement, it then wants to drive the change as fast as possible.

While top management had enough time during the internal debates to buy-in to the planned change, for employees, the planned change is completely new. HR can play an important role in balancing the need of top management for fast execution and time needed for employees to buy-in to the change as well.

Organizational Development

Matthias Zeuch

Get Involved

In organizational development processes, major changes regarding the organizational set-up and/or processes within the company or with its partners be decided. HR has to be part of such processes, bringing in the expertise about the workforce, their competences and emotions.

Develop OD Skills

Organizational development requires both the general skills of Change Management (compare to the respective chapter) and in-depth knowledge about the company. HR leaders should have at least a basic education in organizational development to effectively partner with external consultants. Also, OD skills enhance the general capability of HR to partner with business and drive change within the organization.

M. Zeuch (✉)
Beijing, China
e-mail: DosDontsHR@yahoo.com

© Springer-Verlag Berlin Heidelberg 2015
M. Zeuch (ed.), *Dos and Don'ts in Human Resources Management,*
DOI 10.1007/978-3-662-43553-3_57

Don't Overload Yourself

OD requires both education and practical experience. If you lack either of these, it is not advisable to take over full responsibility for an OD process. This advice is not primarily about the intellectual part of OD, which can be learned via literature, but about the own behavior, particularly in critical and difficult situations.

Also, HR can never be a completely independent facilitator, neutrally analyzing different stakeholder perspectives, because HR is also a stakeholder and has certain interests within the company.

HR Transformation

Christian Weiss

Keep the Ball Rolling

Yes, the role of HR has to be adjusted constantly. Considering the changes in society, technology, business, etc. over the last years, it is surprising how little the HR role and organization has been adjusted and developed. Major corporations have seen more changes, but they are often only superficial. See the opportunities, be bold, take risks! It is only you as HR who can drive this transformation!

Don't Get Stuck in Discussions about the Role of HR

A favorite topic of HR people in transformation workshops is "What is our role?" Since HR has developed the ambition to be more than just the staff administration and payroll processing office of the company, paradigms and buzz-words come and go, which often deal with a customer/business-oriented role or a governance-oriented role. To cut a long story short: "yes" HR has to be customer/service oriented, "yes" it has to take a governance role, and "yes" it has to have a multitude of other roles as well. Determine the role of HR in your organization, but do this together with the business. Clarity of HR accountabilities is critical in the often complex matrix organizations, but avoids getting stuck in these discussions. Focus on real-life topics which matter to the company and do your best to make a valu-

C. Weiss (✉)
Lampertheim, Germany
e-mail: DosDontsHR@yahoo.com

© Springer-Verlag Berlin Heidelberg 2015
M. Zeuch (ed.), *Dos and Don'ts in Human Resources Management*,
DOI 10.1007/978-3-662-43553-3_58

able contribution to them. Define together with the business the type and level of services the internal clients expect from HR. This is essential for the success of the success of HR transformation, but often avoided.

Align the HR Operating Model with the Company Operating Model

Often, the HR operating model hasn't been reviewed when the business strategy and operating model changed. This leads, for example, to a regionally decentralized HR operating model in a company-wide divisionalized organizational set-up. This might still be recommendable from an efficiency point of view (one HR in the countries/regions), but a proper business partnership might require changes to the HR operating model.

Don't Address HR Transformation with Ad-hoc and Single Measures

HR transformation is a longer process with many steps that needs to be planned and executed thoroughly. A holistic approach is required.

It starts with business strategy decode and HR strategy review, continues with HR operating model and structure development, defining of key HR roles and accountabilities, and checking of role fit. It should be accompanied by change management and continuous success measurement activities (HR cockpit of change). Actionism is counterproductive and will confirm the image of HR as not being capable of handling complex projects.

Don't Stay on the Surface

HR transformation requires—as any transformation project—that you roll-out new structures, processes, roles, accountabilities and capabilities not only at the higher levels of the organization. We often see projects that change the HR structures and roles at n-1 and n-2 levels, but leave everything below these managerial layers untouched, assuming that change will just happen here as well—which in reality never does. If an HR transformation shall have a real impact, consistent change has to occur at all levels of the organizations, not only at the top.

Create an Effective HR Top Team

Often, a key element of an HR transformation is the establishment of an effective HR top team. Though HR should be mostly aware of the need of an effective top team, the HR teams we encounter are often quite dysfunctional. You need an engaged and aligned top team and they need to deliver a coherent message, cascaded through the organization in a systematic way. Seventy percent of employees' beliefs are based on observations of the leadership team.

Keep in Mind: "It Takes Two to Tango"

Just by defining for yourself which role you want to have will not change anything. Drive the professionalization of yourself. Use your life experience, your professional experience and accumulate as much knowledge as possible about best practices in HR to come up with the right advice and right decisions. It is highly advisable to rotate through different professional roles (HR and non-HR) to broaden one's scope and to be able to evaluate topics from different relevant perspectives. It is also highly advisable to work in central and de-central parts of the organization! Based on this competence, your partners in business will develop the trust in the capabilities of HR and "allow" you to transform towards being a pro-active, strategic partner.

Labor Cost Reductions / Crisis Management

Matthias Zeuch

Consider Involving Labor Representation Early

In some countries/companies, the involvement of labor representation (unions, internal employee council) is demanded by law or union agreements.

If there is no legal need to do so, it should be discussed whether labor representatives should be involved in the discussion. The answer to this question depends on the level of trust between company leadership and labor representation and the acceptance of labor representatives as opinion leaders within the company. By involving labor representatives, the risk of strikes or forms of passive resistance of the workforce against the to-be-decided measures can be reduced.

Carefully Balance the Burden between Management and Staff

In situations of drastic cost saving measures, people look at fairness of the burden's distribution. If, in addition to significant reductions of their income or benefits, staff feel that "those above" do not really join in with cuts in their income, resistance against the measures will increase, and long-term credibility of the company's management will be at risk.

M. Zeuch (✉)
Beijing, China
e-mail: DosDontsHR@yahoo.com

© Springer-Verlag Berlin Heidelberg 2015
M. Zeuch (ed.), *Dos and Don'ts in Human Resources Management*,
DOI 10.1007/978-3-662-43553-3_59

Clearly Define Scope and Base Line

While the definition of a reduction target is relatively easy (e.g. "All budgets have to be cut by 12 %"), the definition of the scope and the base line can be quite difficult. What if certain parts of the budget are demanded by law? In some countries, for example, cost for employee representation cannot be reduced. Assume that costs for employee representation are part of HR's budget. If HR now has to reduce its overall cost by 12 % but cannot reduce cost for employee representation, the effective savings in the remaining other cost of HR have to be higher. In such cases, it should be considered to take costs, which are demanded by law out of the scope.

Any Definition of a Baseline has its Disadvantages:

If the definition is the original budget plan, which usually has been created some time ago, it can be argued that reality has changed too much to build a good basis for the reduction target. Therefore, discussions about corrections start which are nothing more than exceptions and hence endanger the achievement of the overall reduction target.

If the definition is based on actual spending, there will also be discussions about necessary correction (e.g. due to unplanned one-time costs) and about who was how cost-conscious in the past ("now we get penalized for always having been cost-conscious").

Don't Be Liberal with Exceptions

Exceptions to rules always bear the risk that they erode the rule itself. If you have a general labor cost reduction policy and you make one exception, it is a sure bet that this will stimulate others to also ask for exceptions. In the end, the company runs the risk of not achieving their savings target because many people are busy creating cases for exceptions instead of thinking about ways to save money.

Workforce Planning and Controlling

Christian Weiss

Clear Scope

Workforce planning and controlling can take place at different levels:

1. From more reactive Manpower Planning with a focus on annual budgeting and driven by headcount/FTE and total cost of workforce discussions to
2. Workforce Analytics and Planning based on a workforce architecture (job families/levels) with an understanding of internal and external labor market dynamics and resource availability and finally
3. Strategic Workforce Management and Transformation with a strategically driven understanding of critical roles and strategic capabilities in the organization and evidence-based analytics that supports strategic decision making and drives the strategic people and HR agenda.

It is crucial to clearly determine the level of workforce planning that a company wants to achieve and is able to conduct. Don't aim for levels 2 and 3 if the company doesn't have the needed maturity and systems/processes.

C. Weiss (✉)
Lampertheim, Germany
e-mail: DosDontsHR@yahoo.com

© Springer-Verlag Berlin Heidelberg 2015
M. Zeuch (ed.), *Dos and Don'ts in Human Resources Management*,
DOI 10.1007/978-3-662-43553-3_60

Link to Company Strategy

Ensure that the workforce strategy, model, and KPIs are aligned with the company's strategy, the business model and, if possible, also the operating/governance model. This requires a strategic dialogue between the business leadership and the HR business partners, which is often not conducted or not in a way that properly identifies and converts the business drivers underpinning the business model into strategic capabilities and critical roles. Training and coaching of both sides in the strategic dialogue process is often needed to make it work as business leaders often have problems translating and communicating their strategy to HR, and the HR business partners often lack needed strategic dialogue skills and deep business understanding.

Job Families/Cluster as Basis

Before starting with any workforce modeling, reporting or forecasting, a segmentation of the workforce using a job family modeling/clustering approach is recommended. This enables HR to categorize jobs, conduct reporting on jobs from an additional important structural perspective (other than the organizational) and to focus on those job families where workforce planning is crucial, as they are most critical to strategy implementation.

Job family modeling is an approach to thinking about and structuring work. It aims to categorize work activities to make them easier to manage and describe. A job family clusters related jobs into groups and defines each group in terms of what the jobs within the cluster have in common and what make this group of jobs different from other groups of jobs. A job family is a cluster of jobs that share a specific set of core characteristics and that can be treated as one group.

Focus on Pivotal Roles

Especially in bigger companies, trying to plan and control all jobs in detail will overwhelm HR workforce management. Identifying and focusing on the most critical roles is therefore necessary. This doesn't mean that workforce management shouldn't plan and control less critical roles at all, but major effort should lie on the pivotal roles. Pivotal roles include the following:

- Strategy-critical roles (often roles underpinning strategic capabilities).
- Organization-critical roles (key matrix nodes such as geography leaders intersecting with product leaders).

- Mission-critical (often key roles in operations, difficult/costly to develop/hire).
- Undoable roles.

Identify the Strategic Capabilities

As with pivotal roles also for skills and competencies, a focus is needed, when planning and controlling these in HR: strategic capabilities are the key skills that support the delivery of a company's business model. Some strategic capabilities are generic elements that all companies need to do well as a company, such as innovation or customer-centricity, and some are industry-specific capabilities such as pricing or merchandising in retail. Identifying these capabilities, forecasting and monitoring their demand and supply is vital in order to initiate needed measures to secure the availability (by development or acquisition) of the capabilities when and in the quantity needed by the company. A skill-based approach has shown to be superior to just planning and monitoring the quantity of available and needed roles.

Again, as with pivotal roles, a focus on strategic capabilities doesn't mean that talent management shouldn't address other skills any more. But, most companies are struggling when trying to plan and monitor too many capabilities on a longer term basis.

Get the Data Right

Workforce planning and controlling are very dependent upon the data inputs. Workforce planning often falters, does not achieve the targeted results or requires more time and effort because of data/information issues. The main issues are:

- Overall data availability.
- Quality and consistency of internal data.
- Quality and applicability of external benchmarks/ labor market data.

Already when starting activities to define new reports or introducing strategic workforce planning the availability of data needs to be checked. It is worthwhile investing time to think about the data architecture, ways to collect data and how to maintain and progressively improve this architecture to better reflect workforce planning and controlling needs. Often a lot of time is wasted on trying to collect information which is not necessarily helpful or to define reports or workforce models that can't be filled with needed data.

Collaboration Needed

Workforce planning is not an HR-only exercise. Successful workforce planning is a cooperative effort of different parties, involving business leaders, strategy departments, finance/controlling, HR and often IT. Getting regular buy-in from these stakeholders at every stage of the workforce planning and controlling process is crucial for its success.

Avoid Too Much Complexity

Many companies build in their HR KPI systems or workforce planning models from the start a very high level of complexity to make forecasts as realistic as possible and cover all HR areas. This overwhelms the most organizations, both regarding the needed data to feed the model, which is not easily available, and the amount of variables and its interdependencies. It is highly recommended to increase the complexity over time.

Don't Regard a Spreadsheet as the Right Workforce Planning Tool

Many companies consider spreadsheets like Excel as the tool to use for workforce planning and controlling because of its flexibility and ease of customization. But it has a weak error control, is difficult to inspect and explain, may lead to unit inconsistencies and has a low maintainability. In addition, it offers only poor support for dynamic workforce planning models and simulations. The use of spreadsheets should be limited to the piloting phase, if any.

Mergers–Acquisitions–Joint Ventures

Lynn Schuster and Maureen Hunter

Get Involved Early

In advance of Mergers, Acquisitions and Joint Ventures there are two key phases where HR should be involved early. "Discovery" and "Due Diligence".

During Discovery (before ever setting foot on the ground) HR can research and review information regarding the company culture through the internet, annual reports, press, media and any public information available regarding the acquire. In addition, important information can be gleaned about the senior leadership team from this public information. This helps you to begin to understand potential strengths and challenges the combination may present and aid in the formulation of the most effective integration team to support and enable deal success.

During Due Diligence, it is critical that HR get involved as well. At this point, feasibility and potential for future success is evaluated. To do so, the potential partner companies exchange information and expectations regarding:

- Hard facts (e.g. salary levels and costs of benefits, pension obligations, pending labor law cases with employees, reintegration commitments for employees

L. Schuster (✉)
Wilton, CT, USA
e-mail: DosDontsHR@yahoo.com

M. Hunter
Armonk, NY, USA
e-mail: DosDontsHR@yahoo.com

© Springer-Verlag Berlin Heidelberg 2015
M. Zeuch (ed.), *Dos and Don'ts in Human Resources Management*,
DOI 10.1007/978-3-662-43553-3_61

on foreign assignments/on maternity leave/on military leave, absenteeism rates and average years of service).
- Soft facts (e.g. leadership competencies and potential derailment factors, leadership style, talent pipeline, culture and employee satisfaction).

Soft Aspects Can Become Hard Aspects When They Impact the Bottom Line

Evidence has shown over the years that when soft aspects start to impact the bottom line, they become hard aspects. If they are overlooked, performance lags behind and retention issues begin to surface. In addition, culture clashes can completely derail deal success.

The more complex organizations are, the more important it is to have clarity around all hard and soft aspects in order for leadership to steer the combined organizations in the right direction.

Successful integration and realizing the full potential of the deal is always a challenge.

Take note that in Mergers, Acquisitions and Joint Ventures major challenges exist because many things are new for all involved. In phases when there is lack of transparency and uncertainty, it takes discretionary effort (e.g. stepping in for others, doing things which are not part of the job description, clarifying things, explaining things to others and simply working harder) of all involved to drive the new company to success. If everybody just does what he/she is being told, the odds of failure are high.

Too many open questions regarding the hard facts such as legal issues, financial questions, changes in payroll set-up etc. already capture a lot of capacity on top of the usual day-to-day HR challenges. As a result, HR leaders themselves hardly find the time to deal with the soft aspects. In order to cover both, hard and soft aspects, you have to re-evaluate priorities to determine where it would be advisable to shift priorities or reach out for external support in such situations.

Don't Proclaim Your HR Strategy, Policies and Processes as Being the Only Way Forward

Even though you have good reasons for the way you do HR, the partner side also has good reason for their way.

Early on, you should get in contact with HR of the partner company and try to understand their HR strategy, policies and processes. Particularly in global companies, your HR strategy might not be appropriate in other countries or cultures.

It may be advisable to maintain different HR philosophies in parallel for some time and then to gradually merge those. Obviously, this can mean higher cost compared to a fully integrated solution but the return on investment far outweighs the cost.

Resist the Pull to Assimilate

Look for strengths of both sides and leverage those strengths to integrate for the benefit of the combination.

On a final note, it's important to understand that there is a difference between Mergers, Acquisitions and Joint Ventures. The process may be the same but the emotional impact is different. Acquisitions present the most challenge because people feel like they are losing something. A Merger is a combination of equals and takes place when two businesses wish to become fully integrated. Joint ventures can be a way to test the waters to see if the two entities can work together. Joint ventures can be temporary for a finite period of time.

Never Tell the Acquire that It Will Be Business as Usual

That is like waving a red flag in front of a bull. It never will be business as usual again.

9 783662 435526